A Note From Rick Renner

I am on a personal quest to see a "revival of the Bible" so people can establish their lives on a firm foundation that will stand strong and endure the test as end-time storm winds begin to intensify.

In order to experience a revival of the Bible in your personal life, it is important to take time each day to read, receive, and apply its truths to your life. James tells us that if we will continue in the perfect law of liberty — refusing to be forgetful hearers, but determined to be doers — we will be blessed in our ways. As you watch or listen to the programs in this series and work through this corresponding study guide, I trust you will search the Scriptures and allow the Holy Spirit to help you hear something new from God's Word that applies specifically to your life. I encourage you to be a doer of the Word He reveals to you. Whatever the cost, I assure you — it will be worth it.

> Thy words were found, and I did eat them;
> and thy word was unto me the joy and rejoicing of mine heart:
> for I am called by thy name, O Lord God of hosts.
> — Jeremiah 15:16

Your brother and friend in Jesus Christ,

Rick Renner

How To Use This Study Guide

This ten-lesson study guide corresponds to *"10 Powerful Women" With Rick Renner* (Renner TV). Each lesson in this study guide covers a topic that is addressed during the program series, with questions and references supplied to draw you deeper into your own private study of the Scriptures on this subject.

To derive the most benefit from this study guide, consider the following:

First, watch or listen to the program prior to working through the corresponding lesson in this guide. (Programs can also be viewed at **renner.org** by clicking on the Media/Archives links.)

Second, take the time to look up the scriptures included in each lesson. Prayerfully consider their application to your own life.

Third, use a journal or notebook to make note of your answers to each lesson's Study Questions and Practical Application challenges.

Fourth, invest specific time in prayer and in the Word of God to consult with the Holy Spirit. Write down the scriptures or insights He reveals to you.

Finally, take action! Whatever the Lord tells you to do according to His Word, do it.

For added insights on this subject, it is recommended that you obtain the books *All the Women of the Bible: What Women of the Bible Teach Us Today* by Herbert Lockyer and Rick Renner's autobiography *Unlikely: Our Faith-Filled Journey to the Ends of the Earth*. You may also select from Rick's other available resources by placing your order at **renner.org** or by calling 1-800-742-5593.

TOPIC

Eve — the Mother
of the Human Race

SCRIPTURES

1. **Genesis 2:7-9** — And the Lord God formed man of the dust of the ground, and breathed into his nostrils the breath of life; and man became a living soul. And the Lord God planted a garden eastward in Eden; and there he put the man whom he had formed. And out of the ground made the Lord God to grow every tree that is pleasant to the sight, and good for food; the tree of life also in the midst of the garden, and the tree of knowledge of good and evil.

2. **Genesis 2:15-21** — And the Lord God took the man, and put him into the garden of Eden to dress it and to keep it. And the Lord God commanded the man, saying, Of every tree of the garden thou mayest freely eat: But of the tree of the knowledge of good and evil, thou shalt not eat of it: for in the day that thou eatest thereof thou shalt surely die. And the Lord God said, It is not good that the man should be alone; I will make him an help meet for him. And out of the ground the Lord God formed every beast of the field, and every fowl of the air; and brought them unto Adam to see what he would call them: and whatsoever Adam called every living creature, that was the name thereof. And Adam gave names to all cattle, and to the fowl of the air, and to every beast of the field; but for Adam there was not found an help meet for him. And the Lord God caused a deep sleep to fall upon Adam, and he slept: and he took one of his ribs, and closed up the flesh instead thereof.

3. **1 Peter 3:7** — Likewise, ye husbands, dwell with them according to knowledge, giving honour unto the wife, as unto the weaker vessel, and as being heirs together of the grace of life....

4. **Genesis 2:22-25** — And the rib, which the Lord God had taken from man, made he a woman, and brought her unto the man. And Adam said, This is now bone of my bones, and flesh of my flesh: she shall be called Woman, because she was taken out of Man. Therefore shall

a man leave his father and his mother, and shall cleave unto his wife: and they shall be one flesh. And they were both naked, the man and his wife, and were not ashamed.

5. **Genesis 5:2** — Male and female created he them; and blessed them, and called their name Adam, in the day when they were created.

6. **Genesis 3:20** — …who called his wife's name Eve; because she was the mother of all living.

7. **Genesis 3:1-15** — Now the serpent was more subtil than any beast of the field which the Lord God had made. And he said unto the woman, Yea, hath God said, Ye shall not eat of every tree of the garden? And the woman said unto the serpent, We may eat of the fruit of the trees of the garden: But of the fruit of the tree which is in the midst of the garden, God hath said, Ye shall not eat of it, neither shall ye touch it, lest ye die. And the serpent said unto the woman, Ye shall not surely die. For God doth know that in the day ye eat thereof, then your eyes shall be opened, and ye shall be as gods, knowing good and evil. And when the woman saw that the tree was good for food, and that it was pleasant to the eyes, and a tree to be desired to make one wise, she took of the fruit thereof, and did eat, and gave also unto her husband with her; and he did eat. And the eyes of them both were opened, and they knew that they were naked; and they sewed fig leaves together, and made themselves aprons. And they heard the voice of the Lord God walking in the garden in the cool of the day: and Adam and his wife hid themselves from the presence of the Lord God amongst the trees of the garden. And the Lord God called unto Adam, and said unto him, Where art thou? And he said, I heard thy voice in the garden, and I was afraid, because I was naked; and I hid myself. And he said, Who told thee that thou wast naked? Hast thou eaten of the tree, whereof I commanded thee that thou shouldest not eat? And the man said, The woman whom thou gavest to be with me, she gave me of the tree, and I did eat. And the Lord God said unto the woman, What is this that thou hast done? And the woman said, The serpent beguiled me, and I did eat. And the Lord God said unto the serpent, Because thou hast done this, thou art cursed above all cattle, and above every beast of the field; upon thy belly shalt thou go, and dust shalt thou eat all the days of thy life. And I will put enmity between thee and the woman, and between thy seed and her seed; it shall bruise thy head, and thou shalt bruise his heel.

8. **Genesis 2:16,17** — And the Lord God commanded the man, saying, Of every tree of the garden thou mayest freely eat: but of the tree of the knowledge of good and evil, thou shalt not eat of it: for in the day that thou eatest thereof thou shalt surely die.

9. **Romans 5:12** — Wherefore, as by one man sin entered into the world, and death by sin; and so death passed upon all men, for that all have sinned.

GREEK WORDS

There are no Greek words in this lesson.

SYNOPSIS

The ten lessons in this study on *10 Powerful Women* will focus on the following individuals:

- Eve — the Mother of the Human Race
- Noah's Wife — the Nameless Woman Who Changed History
- Sarah — the Woman God Radically Changed
- Jezebel — the Epitome of an Evil Woman
- Bathsheba — the Adulterer Who Became a Godly Example
- Esther — the Woman Who Saved Her Nation
- Mary — the Mother of Jesus and the Original Pentecostal
- Mary Magdalene — a Woman Who Was Delivered by Jesus
- Mary — a Woman Who Gave Her Living Room to Jesus
- Priscilla — a Woman Preacher

The emphasis of this lesson:

Eve was the first woman, and she was created by God to be Adam's co-partner in life. Initially, man and woman were called Adam and were one in purpose, one in heart. Their choice to disobey God dissolved their unity and opened the door to sin and death. Yet through Eve, God promised redemption.

Women are both beautiful and powerful. Their influence is great in the lives of men, children, and the world itself. The kind of power and influence they have depends on what has happened inside their heart. Women can be manipulative, evil, and controlling, or they can be supportive, godly, helpful, and empowering.

The Bible is full of examples of powerful women — some who used their influence in an evil way and others who used it in a positive way. Both the Old and New Testaments give many examples of women who used their influence correctly to make a positive impact. They were women just like you — facing the same struggles and challenges — but they overcame them and became great influencers.

Adam Was To 'Dress' and 'Keep' the Garden

Eve was the first woman to live on the earth and the first woman mentioned in Scripture. She was created and formed by the very hands of God — a complete and perfect woman. In fact, Eve was the most beautiful woman who ever lived in the world. Like Adam, she was covered and clothed with the glory of God.

Initially, God made Adam. Genesis 2:7-9 says, "And the Lord God formed man of the dust of the ground, and breathed into his nostrils the breath of life; and man became a living soul. And the Lord God planted a garden eastward in Eden; and there he put the man whom he had formed. And out of the ground made the Lord God to grow every tree that is pleasant to the sight, and good for food; the tree of life also in the midst of the garden, and the tree of knowledge of good and evil."

Once man was created, Scripture says, "And the Lord God took the man, and put him into the garden of Eden to dress it and to keep it" (Genesis 2:15). The words "dress it" means *to cultivate and develop it*. As perfect as Eden was, God expected man to take it to a higher level. This principle of improvement has been in place since the beginning. Whatever God places in our hands — our marriages, our children, our businesses — we are to make better.

In addition to dressing the garden, God also appointed Adam to "keep it." The original meaning here in Hebrew means *to keep it from danger*. The use of this wording lets us know that God had informed Adam that there was an evil presence outside the garden that would try to find his way into the garden. This predator's name was — and *is* — Satan. Since Adam was head of the garden, God needed to inform him of this arch enemy. Adam understood it was his God-given responsibility to obey God and protect the garden and thereby keep the devil out of Eden.

Make no mistake. Adam understood his assignment because God — the Master Communicator — clearly delivered the instructions. Adding to this, the Bible says, "And the Lord God commanded the man, saying, Of every tree of the garden thou mayest freely eat: But of the tree of the knowledge of good and evil, thou shalt not eat of it: for in the day that thou eatest thereof thou shalt surely die" (Genesis 2:16,17).

Disobedience to this commandment would open the door to the devil and allow him to enter the garden and flood the earth with death and destruction (*see* Romans 5:14,17).

Eve Was Created To Be Adam's Co-partner

Immediately after downloading these instructions to Adam, "…The Lord God said, It is not good that the man should be alone; I will make him an help meet for him" (Genesis 2:18). The words "help meet" in Hebrew literally mean *one adapted to him*. God described the woman as Adam's "help meet," which is a picture of *partnership*.

It is crucial for all of us to realize that *in Christ*, women become co-rulers or co-partners with their spouses. That is the implication we find in this phrase "help meet." In lands where the Gospel is stifled and darkness reigns, women are often treated as slaves. But in Christ, women are elevated to a co-ruler, co-partnership position with their spouse. This is what God gave Eve. Together, Eve and Adam's heart beat as one.

Genesis 2:19 and 20 go on to say, "And out of the ground the Lord God formed every beast of the field, and every fowl of the air; and brought them unto Adam to see what he would call them: and whatsoever Adam called every living creature, that was the name thereof. And Adam gave names to all cattle, and to the fowl of the air, and to every beast of the field; but for Adam there was not found an help meet for him."

As Adam was busy about his work naming all the animals, he noticed that each species came in pairs. Adam looked and looked, but he couldn't find a counterpart to be his mate. *Where's mine?* he must have asked. To effectively deal with this dilemma, the Bible says, "And the Lord God caused a deep sleep to fall upon Adam, and he slept: and he took one of his ribs, and closed up the flesh instead thereof" (Genesis 2:21).

Isn't that interesting? As Adam *rested* in the Lord, the Lord Himself went to work on Adam's problem, creating a solution that Adam couldn't even put into words. Under supernatural anesthesia, God performed the first surgery and birthed woman out of man. Specifically, He took one of Adam's "ribs" — which in the original Hebrew means a *part of his side* — and He formed the substance into a refined female.

Why was part of Adam's side used? As one anonymous source has said, "She was not made out of his head to *surpass* him, nor from his feet to be *trampled* on, but from his side to be *equal* to him, and near his heart to be *dear* to him." God created a help mate for Adam that was his equal partner who would co-rule the earth with him. They were to be heirs together of the grace of life.

First Peter 3:7 confirms this, saying, "Likewise, ye husbands, dwell with them according to knowledge, giving honour unto the wife, as unto the weaker vessel, and as being heirs together of the grace of life...." Now, while some have said that the words "weaker vessel" signify that women are inferior to men, that is not what it means. The phrase "weaker vessel" describes a treasured vessel that is fragile and should be treated as precious and priceless. God's intention from the very beginning was for the man and his wife to be coheirs of the grace of God — not rivals competing for the top position.

Initially, Adam and Eve Together Were Called 'Adam'

Returning to the Genesis account, it says, "And the rib, which the Lord God had taken from man, made he a woman, and brought her unto the man" (Genesis 2:22). Again, we see the word "rib," which actually describes *a part of Adam's side*. The Lord took Adam's flesh and bone and "made" — which literally means *constructed* — Eve. Then He "brought her" to Adam. The word "brought" in the original language describes *a magnificent presentation*. God built the most beautiful woman in human history and presented her to Adam.

"And Adam said, This is now bone of my bones, and flesh of my flesh: she shall be called Woman, because she was taken out of Man" (Genesis 2:23). The original Hebrew word for "woman" here means having *the likeness of man*. Although Eve was like Adam, she had her unique differences.

Genesis 5:2 declares, "Male and female created he them; and blessed them, and called their name Adam, in the day when they were created."

In the beginning, God gave the first man and first woman *one name.* Adam and Eve together were called "Adam." They had *one identity* — and maintained it — until the fall. This shows God's plan for unity in marriage. Genesis 2:24 and 25 says, "Therefore shall a man leave his father and his mother, and shall cleave unto his wife: and they shall be *one flesh.* And they were both naked, the man and his wife, and were not ashamed." Again, Adam and Eve were dressed in the glory of God. They didn't need clothing because God Himself was their covering.

Eve's separate identity didn't emerge until after sin entered the world. That was the point at which she began to feel separation from her husband's authority and when tension began between them. None of that existed before sin came. Genesis 3:20 says, "And Adam called his wife's name Eve; because she was the mother of all living." The name Eve was given to her by Adam *after* they disobeyed God and sinned. It was Adam's choice.

Adam and Eve Were Equally at Fault for the Fall

As you probably know, Eve has taken the rap for the fall for thousands of years. But was she the only one at fault? What was Adam's role in everything? Let's take the next few moments to unpack Genesis 3 and get a better, clearer perspective of what actually took place that day. The Bible says:

> **Now the serpent was more subtil than any beast of the field which the Lord God had made. And he said unto the woman, Yea, hath God said, Ye shall not eat of every tree of the garden? And the woman said unto the serpent, We may eat of the fruit of the trees of the garden: but of the fruit of the tree which is in the midst of the garden, God hath said, Ye shall not eat of it, neither shall ye touch it, lest ye die.**
>
> **— Genesis 3:1-3**

Notice the words "neither shall ye touch it." Is that actually what God said to Adam? Genesis 2:17 records God as saying, "But of the tree of the knowledge of good and evil, *thou shalt not eat of it:* for in the day that thou eatest thereof thou shalt surely die." Somehow Eve misunderstood the instructions. In her mind, she thought they were forbidden to even "touch" the fruit of the tree of the knowledge of good and evil. Somehow she thought the tree was poisonous or fatal to their physical lives.

The reason Eve misinterpreted God's command is apparently because Adam — who was the head of the home — failed to communicate it to her correctly. The issue was not about avoiding poisonous fruit — the issue was obeying or not obeying God's spoken word. Hence, the devil found an entryway into the lives of man through ignorance.

The Bible says, "And the serpent said unto the woman, Ye shall not surely die: For God doth know that in the day ye eat thereof, then your eyes shall be opened, and ye shall be as gods, knowing good and evil. And when the woman saw that the tree was good for food, and that it was pleasant to the eyes, and a tree to be desired to make one wise, she took of the fruit thereof, and did eat, and gave also unto her husband with her; and he did eat" (Genesis 3:4-6).

So while it appears Eve sinned out of ignorance, Adam sinned with the full knowledge of what God had said. Which begs the question, why would Adam blatantly disobey? It seems he knew if he didn't join her, he would lose her. If he remained pure and she was in sin, they would be unequally yoked; and she would die and he would go on living. Adam could not bear the thought of losing his soul mate. Therefore, he willingly reached out and ate what he knew he wasn't supposed to eat.

Our Actions Have Consequences

Immediately after Adam and Eve disobeyed God, the Bible says:

> …The eyes of them both were opened, and they knew that they were naked; and they sewed fig leaves together, and made themselves aprons.
>
> And they heard the voice of the Lord God walking in the garden in the cool of the day: and Adam and his wife hid themselves from the presence of the Lord God amongst the trees of the garden.
>
> And the Lord God called unto Adam, and said unto him, Where art thou? And he said, I heard thy voice in the garden, and I was afraid, because I was naked; and I hid myself.

**And he said, Who told thee that thou wast naked? Hast thou
eaten of the tree, whereof I commanded thee that thou shouldest not eat?**

**And the man said, The woman whom thou gavest to be with me,
she gave me of the tree, and I did eat.**
                                                    — Genesis 3:7-12

One of the first side effects of sin is pointing a finger of blame. When
God called Adam to give an answer for his actions, Adam not only
blamed his wife for giving him the fruit, but he also blamed God for
giving him Eve. Nevertheless, God held Adam accountable first. This is
why Paul wrote:

**Wherefore, as by one man sin entered into the world, and
death by sin; and so death passed upon all men, for that all have
sinned.**
                                                    — Romans 5:12

The first person God went to when Adam and Eve disobeyed was Adam,
not Eve. Eve is not even mentioned in Romans 5:12. Adam was the head
of the household, which made him ultimately responsible. However, Eve
was not off the hook. The Bible says:

**And the Lord God said unto the woman, What is this that thou
hast done? And the woman said, The serpent beguiled me, and
I did eat.**
                                                    — Genesis 3:13

Would Eve have been beguiled had she fully understood what God had
said? Possibly not.

Interestingly, after questioning both Adam and Eve about their actions,
God turned and immediately pronounced judgment on the serpent:

**And the Lord God said unto the serpent, Because thou hast
done this, thou art cursed above all cattle, and above every
beast of the field; upon thy belly shalt thou go, and dust shalt
thou eat all the days of thy life.**
                                                    — Genesis 3:14

God Promised a Redeemer!

The very first prophecy concerning the coming of the Messiah is in Genesis 3:15. God Himself declared a Redeemer would come to defeat the work of the devil. He said, "And I will put enmity between thee and the woman, and between thy seed and her seed; it shall bruise thy head, and thou shalt bruise his heel."

This is a snapshot of Eve's story — the world's first woman who was perfect and most powerful. Yet, she was beguiled. She made a mistake because of flawed information, but God was there from the beginning to bail her and her husband out of the mess they had made. Through her, God promised to send a redeemer, and that Redeemer is Jesus Christ!

STUDY QUESTIONS

Study to shew thyself approved unto God, a workman that needeth not to be ashamed, rightly dividing the word of truth.
— 2 Timothy 2:15

1. What new insights did you learn about Eve, the first woman? How about Adam?
2. Take a moment to review the section on the fall, and in your own words, explain where both Adam and Eve went wrong. What should each of them have done differently?
3. Slowly read through Genesis 3:7-12 and identify the side effects of sin entering the world. How did man respond — to their situation, to each other, and to God? What is the Holy Spirit showing you personally in this passage?

PRACTICAL APPLICATION

But be ye doers of the word, and not hearers only, deceiving your own selves.
— James 1:22

1. The principle of improvement has been in place since the beginning of time. God wants us to take what He's placed in our hands — our marriages, our children, our businesses, etc. — and continue to make them better. What has God specifically placed in your hands that you

know He wants to improve? How can you work with His Spirit to help bring this about?

2. In Christ, women become *co-rulers* or *co-partners* with their husbands. That is the meaning of the words "help meet" in Genesis 2:18. Men, be honest. Do you treat your wife as a co-partner or co-ruler in your marriage? What evidence can you offer to back up your answer?

3. As Adam *rested* in the Lord, the Lord Himself went to work on Adam's problem, creating a solution that Adam couldn't even put into words. Is there something you have been working feverishly to try and fix, but nothing seems to change? If so, what is it? And what does the example of the creation of Eve speak to you about your situation?

4. Like Adam and Eve, have you made mistakes that brought about grave consequences? If you'll turn to God in repentance, He'll take your situation and turn it around for good. Take time now to confess any sin and ask for His forgiveness, surrendering yourself and your situation to Him.

LESSON 2

TOPIC

Noah's Wife — the Nameless Woman Who Changed History

SCRIPTURES

1. **Genesis 6:8-12** — But Noah found grace in the eyes of the Lord. These are the generations of Noah: Noah was a just man and perfect in his generations, and Noah walked with God. And Noah begat three sons, Shem, Ham, and Japheth. The earth also was corrupt before God, and the earth was filled with violence. And God looked upon the earth, and, behold, it was corrupt; for all flesh had corrupted his way upon the earth.

2. **Hebrews 11:7** — By faith Noah, being warned of God of things not seen as yet, moved with fear, prepared an ark to the saving of his house; by the which he condemned the world, and became heir of the righteousness which is by faith.

3. **Genesis 7:6,7,13** — And Noah was six hundred years old when the flood of waters was upon the earth. And Noah went in, and his sons, and his wife, and his sons' wives with him, into the ark, because of the waters of the flood. …In the selfsame day entered Noah, and Shem, and Ham, and Japheth, the sons of Noah, and Noah's wife, and the three wives of his sons with them, into the ark.

4. **Genesis 8:15-21** — And God spake unto Noah, saying, Go forth of the ark, thou, and thy wife, and thy sons, and thy sons' wives with thee. Bring forth with thee every living thing that is with thee, of all flesh, both of fowl, and of cattle, and of every creeping thing that creepeth upon the earth; that they may breed abundantly in the earth, and be fruitful, and multiply upon the earth. And Noah went forth, and his sons, and his wife, and his sons' wives with him: Every beast, every creeping thing, and every fowl, and whatsoever creepeth upon the earth, after their kinds, went forth out of the ark. And Noah builded an altar unto the Lord; and took of every clean beast, and of every clean fowl, and offered burnt offerings on the altar. And the Lord smelled a sweet savour; and the Lord said in his heart, I will not again curse the ground any more for man's sake; for the imagination of man's heart is evil from his youth; neither will I again smite any more every thing living as I have done.

5. **Genesis 9:28,29** — And Noah lived after the flood three hundred and fifty years. And all the days of Noah were nine hundred and fifty years: and he died.

GREEK WORDS

1. "not seen as yet" — **μηδέπω** (*medepo*): not yet, never before

2. "moved with fear" — **εὐλαβέομαι** (*eulabeomai*): to take action urgently and seriously

3. "prepared" — **κατασκευάζω** (*kataskeuadzo*): he put forth effort to build a vessel, an ark

4. "to the saving of his house" — **εἰς σωτηρίαν τοῦ οἴκου αὐτοῦ** (*eis soterian tou oikou autou*): for the explicit purpose of saving his own household

SYNOPSIS

When God calls a man and woman together to be husband and wife, He is uniting two people with two sets of gifts to do something far greater than either could do on their own. Every marriage He ordains has great purpose — to birth godly children and advance God's kingdom in the earth on multiple levels.

If you think about it, behind just about every successful, godly man is a godly wife. Instead of selfishly trying to manipulate and control her husband, she is supportive and helpful to him in fulfilling his calling. One such woman lived during Old Testament times, and while we don't know her name, we do know that she changed history. We are talking about *Noah's wife*.

The emphasis of this lesson:

Noah's wife played a powerful role in helping to preserve her family — and the human race — through the most catastrophic time in world history. Although she's nameless, it does not diminish her vital contribution of support to her husband, her sons, and her sons' wives.

The World in Noah's Day
Was Corrupt Beyond Belief

Noah's wife is the nameless woman who changed history. Although the Bible doesn't offer much information on her life, there are certainly some characteristics about her that we can determine. Noah's story begins in the sixth chapter of Genesis. When the world was saturated with sin and every thought and imagination of men's hearts was continually evil, the Bible says:

> **But Noah found grace in the eyes of the Lord. These are the generations of Noah: Noah was a just man and perfect in his generations, and Noah walked with God. And Noah begat three sons, Shem, Ham, and Japheth.**
>
> **— Genesis 6:8-10**

If you read between the lines, you can conclude that Noah had a wife, and it was his wife that actually gave birth to his three sons Shem, Ham, and Japheth. What kind of environment did Mr. and Mrs. Noah's sons grow up in? Genesis 6:11 and 12 says, "The earth also was corrupt before God, and the earth was filled with violence. And God looked upon the earth, and, behold, it was corrupt; for all flesh had corrupted his way upon the earth."

Can you imagine the pressures on this family? As they gave their all to living pure and godly lives, outside forces to conform to the ways of the world were constantly pushing against their souls. Yet they determined to take the high road and live righteously and holy each day before God. And the dedication and devotion of Noah and his wife caught the attention of the Most High.

God Warned Noah of What Was Coming

In His mercy, God told Noah, "…The end of all flesh is come before me; for the earth is filled with violence through them; and, behold, I will destroy them with the earth" (Genesis 6:13).

What's interesting is that Hebrews 11:7 confirms this forewarning from God, saying, "By faith Noah, being warned of God of things not seen as yet, moved with fear, prepared an ark to the saving of his house; by the which he condemned the world, and became heir of the righteousness which is by faith."

Notice the phrase "not seen as yet." This is a translation of the Greek word *medepo*, and it specifically means *not yet* or *never before*. Up until that point in time, no one had ever heard of or seen a flood. In fact, Scripture suggests that before the great deluge, it hadn't even rained. Instead, a mist came up from the ground and watered the whole earth (*see* Genesis 2:6). Noah and his wife and his sons believed that a flood was coming — just as God said — even though they had never seen a flood in their lives.

When God warned Noah and his wife of what was coming, Noah was "moved with fear." This phrase is a translation of the Greek word *eulabeomai*, which means *to take action urgently and very seriously*. What action did Noah take? He "…prepared an ark to the saving of his house…" (Hebrews 11:7). The word "prepared" is the Greek word *kataskeuadzo*, and it means Noah *put forth effort to build a vessel*, an ark — effort that took nearly 100 years. He did it in obedience to God and "to the saving of his house," which in Greek literally means *for the explicit purpose of saving his own household*.

A Time of Building and Waiting

The Bible informs us that when Noah was 500 years old, he and his wife became the parents of Shem, Ham, and Japheth (*see* Genesis 5:32). Although it is not certain, it is possible that these three sons were triplets. About 100 years later, when Noah was 600 years of age, the fountains of the deep were broken up and the rain began to fall (*see* Genesis 7:11). At some point early on during those hundred years, Noah received the assignment to build the ark.

Meanwhile, Noah and his wife taught their sons — and eventually their sons' wives — about God and how to live righteously in their perverse generation. They did whatever was necessary to hold their family together and to walk holy before the Lord, regardless of the ridicule or pressures against them.

As the years passed, they continued to build the ark and wait for God to fulfill what He had spoken. They used their own resources and invested tremendous effort and energy into the project. As a family, they stayed focused, and they stood together against every challenge. They believed and trusted the word God had spoken to Noah.

It's likely that there were financial challenges along the way, and that people laughed at Noah, his wife, and his sons quite a bit. Did people in the community vandalize the job site? Did they ridicule Noah and his family and make up all kinds of nasty, derogatory jokes? It's almost a certainty. Remember, there had never been a flood, so it's doubtful that anyone understood what was coming. Yet, Noah's wife, his sons, and his sons' wives quietly followed and submitted to Noah and carried out the task God had asked of them.

Noah's Wife Was Apparently a Source of Strength

Throughout the entire ordeal, Noah's wife could have questioned him. She could have argued about the money he was spending. She could have alleged that he was destroying their sons' future. After all, she was not the one who heard from God. More than likely, there were times when Noah's wife asked, "Noah, are you absolutely sure God asked you to do this?" Possibly even his sons said, "Dad, we're giving our lives for this project. Do you know without question that God has spoken to you?"

Keep in mind that the Bible identifies Noah as "a preacher of righteousness" (*see* 2 Peter 2:5). He was a prophet who prophesied a worldwide flood was coming that was going to destroy the earth and everything in it. Again, people had never heard of or seen a flood, and they had never seen an ark being built — or the parade of animals that eventually gathered in Noah's community and came into the ark. Indeed, these things seemed extremely bizarre to all the bystanders.

Undoubtedly, there were forces all around Noah pulling on him and trying to move him out of his place of faith. Yet, regardless of the world's criticism, the questions from his family, and even the personal concerns that weighed on his own mind, Noah stuck with God's plan. And apparently, his wife stayed right by his side, supporting and encouraging him through everything. She could either hinder or help him. It seems she chose to do the latter. If Noah and his wife fought and argued, the Bible doesn't tell us.

The Flood Finally Arrived

Scripture goes on to say, "And Noah was six hundred years old when the flood of waters was upon the earth. And Noah went in, and his sons, and his wife, and his sons' wives with him, into the ark because of the waters of the flood" (Genesis 7:6,7).

Did you ever stop to think about how Shem, Ham, and Japheth's wives were watching Noah's wife? They needed her godly example and looked to their mother-in-law to show them how to do things right. Imagine if these three younger women would have observed their mother-in-law arguing frequently with their father-in-law Noah. It would have made the girls question if their husbands were doing right or wrong. But there is no record of such things happening.

Interestingly, the Bible says, "In the selfsame day entered Noah, and Shem, and Ham, and Japheth, the sons of Noah, and Noah's wife, and the three wives of his sons with them, into the ark" (Genesis 7:13). It was on that same day that all the animals came to Noah and entered the ark (*see* Genesis 7:14). Once Noah and his wife, his sons and their wives, and all the animals were inside, the Bible says, "And it came to pass after seven days, that the waters of the flood were upon the earth" (Genesis 7:10).

We know from Scripture that it rained nonstop for 40 days and 40 nights, and that the flood waters prevailed — which means they *continued to rise and dominate* — on the earth for 150 days (*see* Genesis 7:12 and 24). By the time the flood waters had receded, Noah and his wife and his sons and their wives were on the ark with all the animals for 375 days!

Exiting the Ark

What happened to Noah and his family after their year-long voyage? Genesis 8:15-19 says:

> **And God spake unto Noah, saying, Go forth of the ark, thou, and thy wife, and thy sons, and thy sons' wives with thee. Bring forth with thee every living thing that is with thee, of all flesh, both of fowl, and of cattle, and of every creeping thing that creepeth upon the earth; that they may breed abundantly in the earth, and be fruitful, and multiply upon the earth. And Noah went forth, and his sons, and his wife, and his sons' wives with him: Every beast, every creeping thing, and every fowl, and whatsoever creepeth upon the earth, after their kinds, went forth out of the ark.**

What was the very first thing Noah did once the ship had disembarked and unloaded? The Bible says, "And Noah builded an altar unto the Lord; and took of every clean beast, and of every clean fowl, and offered burnt offerings on the altar. And the Lord smelled a sweet savour; and the Lord said in his heart, I will not again curse the ground any more for man's sake; for the imagination of man's heart is evil from his youth; neither will I again smite any more every thing living as I have done" (Genesis 8:20,21).

Where was Noah's wife when Noah built the altar and worshiped the Lord with the sacrifices? She was probably right by her husband's side worshipping with him.

Did you ever stop to think about the condition of the earth after the flood? The devastation left behind by a year of out-of-control flood waters that covered the highest mountains must have been staggering. Nothing looked like it did prior to the flood, that's for sure. In many places, it must have been one big muddy mess.

Again, Noah's wife could have complained, "Is this what we sacrificed and worked years and years to prepare for? Is this what we stayed on that ark for after a year with all those smelly animals?" How horribly difficult would it have been for Noah had his wife been argumentative and uncooperative? If there were any complaints from Mrs. Noah or the wives of her sons, we have no record of it. It appears that Noah's wife was supportive of her husband and the call on his life.

Scripture goes on to say, "And God blessed Noah and his sons, and said unto them, Be fruitful and multiply, and replenish the earth" (Genesis 9:1). Thus, not only did Shem, Ham, and Japheth and their wives repopulate the earth, but so did Noah and his wife. "And Noah lived after the flood three hundred and fifty years. And all the days of Noah were nine hundred and fifty years: and he died" (Genesis 9:28,29). Noah lived 600 years before the flood and 350 years after the flood for a grand total of 950 fulfilling years on the earth.

In our next lesson, we will examine the life of Sarah, the wife of Abraham, and learn how God radically changed her from being an argumentative complainer into the mother of faith.

STUDY QUESTIONS

Study to shew thyself approved unto God, a workman that needeth not to be ashamed, rightly dividing the word of truth.
— 2 Timothy 2:15

1. What new things did you learn about Noah's wife, the nameless woman who changed history? How is this lesson helping you see her in a way you've never seen her before?
2. If you were Mrs. Noah living in those days, what do you think your greatest challenge would have been before the flood? How about after the flood?
3. According to Genesis 6:1-12, what were the conditions of the world during Noah's day? How did people treat each other? What did Jesus say about the days of Noah in Luke 17:26,27?

PRACTICAL APPLICATION

But be ye doers of the word, and not hearers only, deceiving your own selves.
— James 1:22

1. Imagine you were Noah and God gave you the assignment to build the ark to save your family. How difficult would it have been for you to accomplish your work if your wife would have been argumenta-

tive and uncooperative? How do you think her attitude would have affected your sons and their wives?

2. If you are married, do you support your husband and the call on his life? If you were to ask him — and he answered you truthfully — would he say he feels your *support* or that you *fight against him*?

3. Is it possible that God hasn't given him a bigger assignment because He knows you wouldn't support him? OR are you and your attitude one of the reasons God knows He can give your husband a big assignment?

LESSON 3

TOPIC

Sarah — the Woman God Radically Changed

SCRIPTURES

1. **Genesis 12:1** — …Get thee out of thy country, and from thy kindred, and from thy father's house, unto a land that I will shew thee.

2. **Genesis 12:5** — And Abraham took Sarai his wife, and Lot his brother's son, and all their substance that they had gathered, and the souls that they had gotten in Haran; and they went forth to go into the land of Canaan; and into the land of Canaan they came.

3. **Genesis 17:1** — And when Abram was ninety years old and nine, the Lord appeared to Abram, and said unto him, I am the Almighty God; walk before me, and be thou perfect.

4. **Genesis 18:9-15** — And they said unto him, Where is Sarah thy wife? And he said, Behold, in the tent. And he said, I will certainly return unto thee according to the time of life; and, lo, Sarah thy wife shall have a son. And Sarah heard it in the tent door, which was behind him. Now Abraham and Sarah were old and well stricken in age; and it ceased to be with Sarah after the manner of women. Therefore Sarah laughed within herself, saying, After I am waxed old shall I have pleasure, my Lord being old also? And the Lord said unto Abraham, Wherefore did Sarah laugh, saying, Shall I of a surety bear

a child, which am old? Is any thing too hard for the Lord? At the time appointed I will return unto thee, according to the time of life, and Sarah shall have a son. Then Sarah denied, saying, I laughed not; for she was afraid. And he said, Nay; but thou didst laugh.

5. **Isaiah 51:1-2** — Hearken to me, ye that follow after righteousness, ye that seek the Lord: look unto the rock whence ye are hewn, and unto the hole of the pit whence ye are digged. Look unto Abraham your father, and unto Sarah that bare you….

6. **1 Peter 3:3-6** — Whose adorning let it not be that outward adorning of plaiting the hair, and of wearing of gold, or of putting on of apparel; But let it be the hidden man of the heart, in that which is not corruptible, even the ornament of a meek and quiet spirit, which is in the sight of God of great price. For after this manner in the old time the holy women also, who trusted in God, adorned themselves, being in subjection unto their own husbands: Even as Sara obeyed Abraham, calling him lord: whose daughters ye are, as long as ye do well, and are not afraid with any amazement.

GREEK WORDS

1. "obeyed" — ὑπακούω (*hupakouo*): from ὑπό (*hupo*): and ἀκούω (*akouo*): the word ὑπό (*hupo*): means under, and ἀκούω (*akouo*): means I hear; compounded, to come under one's authority and to open the ears to hear and to follow what is being communicated

2. "Lord" — κύριος (*kurios*): Lord, or supreme master

SYNOPSIS

In Lesson 1, we learned about Eve, the very first woman created directly by the hands of God. She was flawless and lived in a perfect environment. Yet she — along with Adam — made a costly mistake that opened the door for Satan to enter the human race, bringing death and destruction. In spite of her choice to disobey God, the Lord redeemed her situation.

In our second lesson, we looked at Noah's wife — the nameless woman who changed history. It appears that this powerful woman stood supportively by her husband's side as he and their sons labored intensely for years on end to build the ark that would deliver their family. Rather than complain and question Noah's every move, it seems Mrs. Noah helped to raise their sons to live pure and righteous lives. After the flood, she and

Noah and their sons and their sons' wives became the progenitors of the human race.

Our next powerful woman in Scripture we want to look at is Sarah, the wife of Abraham. Although she is often remembered as the beautiful princess who was the mother of faith, her demeanor when God first called Abraham was not as charming and compliant as you may think.

The emphasis of this lesson:

Although outwardly Sarai was breathtakingly beautiful, inwardly she was very unpleasant and hard to get along with. God radically transformed her from a critical, unsupportive, and sarcastic woman into *Sarah*, His princess who supported and submitted to Abraham's authority.

Abram's First Encounter With God

Abram and Sarai — which were their names originally — lived a very lavish, self-focused life in the land of Ur of Chaldees before the Lord called Abram to leave his home and follow Him. They had no children and likely served the moon god that was worshiped by most people living in the land of Mesopotamia.

Then one day Abram encountered God. The Bible says, "…The God of glory appeared unto our father Abraham, when he was in Mesopotamia, before he dwelt in Charran, And said unto him, Get thee out of thy country, and from thy kindred, and come into the land which I shall shew thee" (Acts 7:2,3). This is the same calling we see documented in Genesis 12:1.

The word "appeared" here is the Greek word *phaneros*, and it describes *something that suddenly manifests*. On that day, God somehow, someway unexpectedly manifested His presence to Abram in a misty cloud of His glory, and that glory enveloped him. From within that cloud, God preached to Abram the message of the Gospel hundreds of years before Jesus was even born (*see* Galatians 3:8). In that moment, Abram believed God and surrendered his life to Him.

We might describe that day as the day Abram was "saved." There was only one problem: Sarai was not with Abram when he met God, nor did she hear His voice. When Abram returned home after his encounter with God and announced that he and Sarai would be leaving their rich and comfortable life to follow God, she was likely very resistant. Although she and Abram were married, they had become unequally yoked spiritually.

What Does the Name 'Sarai' Mean?

You may be aware that the name "Sarah" means *princess*. What you may not know is the meaning of the name "Sarai." If we dig a little deeper into the Hebrew origins of this name, we will discover that "Sarai" is derived from the word for *quarrelsome* or *contentious*. Thus, Sarai's name seems to signify *one who is a complainer or griper*. Although outwardly she was breathtakingly beautiful, inwardly she was very unpleasant and difficult to be around.

Make no mistake. Before God transformed Sarai, she was anything but congenial. A careful read through the book of Genesis reveals that she was critical, unsupportive, and sarcastic many times. She even had the audacity to argue with God.

When Abram came and told Sarai that the Lord appeared to him and said, "…Get thee out of thy country, and from thy kindred, and from thy father's house, unto a land that I will shew thee" (Genesis 12:1), it is very likely that Sarai pushed back. Living up to her name as one who is contentious and quarrelsome, she probably said something like, "What? We're going *where*, to do *what*? You're taking me away from this luxurious palace to go live in a tent? Your God didn't speak to me, so I'm not going."

Why would we say Sarai likely responded in this way? The answer is in Genesis 12:5, which says, "And Abram *took* Sarai his wife…and they went forth to go into the land of Canaan; and into the land of Canaan they came." The word "took" here implies that Sarai was uncooperative and did not willingly accompany Abram. There may have even been a huge fight. Why might have Sarai been resistant?

Abram Often Made Glaring Errors

The Bible does not hide the fact that Abram was a man who made many mistakes — even *after* he encountered God and began following Him. For instance:

- He went to Egypt instead of staying in the land of promise where God told him to go (*see* Genesis 12:10).

- He indirectly asked Sarai to sleep with the Egyptian king when he asked her to lie and say she was just his sister (*see* Genesis 12:11-13).

- He committed adultery when he slept with Hagar (*see* Genesis 16:2-4).

- He became the father of Ishmael, creating a serious family problem (*see* Genesis 16 and 21).

And the list goes on, and on, and on. The fact is, Abram made so many mistakes that God pulled him aside one day to talk about it. Genesis 17:1 says, "And when Abram was ninety years old and nine, the Lord appeared to Abram, and said unto him, I am the Almighty God; walk before me, and be thou perfect."

Basically, God told Abram, "Hey, get it together. Quit making foolish decisions." Well, if God saw Abram's blunders and called him on it, Sarai likely saw them too — but was not nearly as patient or gracious. Consequently, it may have been very difficult for her to submit to his leadership.

Sarai Was Contentious and Sarcastic

As we noted, the name "Sarai" signifies *one who complains and is quarrelsome*. Even after God changed her name to *Sarah*, this feisty, argumentative attitude was still evident at times. A great example of this is seen in how she interacted with a very special guest who visited her and Abram at their camp. The Bible says that the Lord Himself appeared to Abraham when he and Sarah were living in the plains of Mamre (*see* Genesis 18:1). After Abraham served a delicious meal to the Lord and the two angels who were with Him, the Bible says:

> **And they said unto him, Where is Sarah thy wife? And he said, Behold, in the tent.**
>
> **And he said, I will certainly return unto thee according to the time of life; and, lo, Sarah thy wife shall have a son. And Sarah heard it in the tent door, which was behind him.**
>
> **Now Abraham and Sarah were old and well stricken in age; and it ceased to be with Sarah after the manner of women.**
>
> **Therefore Sarah laughed within herself, saying, After I am waxed old shall I have pleasure, my Lord being old also?**

And the Lord said unto Abraham, Wherefore did Sarah laugh, saying, Shall I of a surety bear a child, which am old?

Is any thing too hard for the Lord? At the time appointed I will return unto thee, according to the time of life, and Sarah shall have a son.

Then Sarah denied, saying, I laughed not; for she was afraid. And he said, Nay; but thou didst laugh.
— Genesis 18:9-15

Essentially, Sarah was eavesdropping on Abraham's conversation with the Lord, and when she overheard Him promise to give her a child of her own body, she laughed. In great disbelief, she sarcastically said to herself, *"Yeah, right! Like I'm going to have a baby at my age! There's just no way."*

The Lord heard Sarah laugh and then repeated to Abraham the very thoughts Sarah was thinking to herself. He then repeated His promise that she would give birth to a child. At that point, Sarah piped up from inside the tent and emphatically denied that she laughed. The Lord then called her on her actions saying, "Oh, but you *did* laugh!"

Think about it. Sarah had the nerve to laugh at what the Lord said and then argue with Him about what she did and didn't say. If she was quarrelsome and sarcastic with Almighty God, the chances are pretty good that she was just as cynical and argumentative with Abraham on occasion.

Over time, Sarah's demeanor did soften after she encountered God for herself and she held in her hands the promised blessing of Isaac — the child of her own body. When the Lord changed Abram's name to *Abraham*, He also changed Sarai's name to *Sarah*. She went from being the *griping, complaining, quarrelsome one* to being God's *princess*! Little by little, she learned to submit to and respect Abraham — even with his many faults and flaws.

Practical Instruction for Husbands and Wives

Men, we need to do all we can to make it easier for our wives to submit to and follow our leadership. It makes sense why some wives don't want to follow their husbands. They have witnessed them make reckless decisions and do foolish things. They have started projects they didn't finish, operated in pride, and been unstable. When these same men ask their wives to get on board with the "new thing" they want to do, their wives are very reluctant. As men we need to walk in humility, always seek the wisdom of God, and remain stable and godly in all we do.

At the same time, wives need to do all they can to be easy to lead. This would include things like being respectful and honoring, cooperative and submissive, loving and thankful. As a wife, if you're griping, complaining, arguing, and being sarcastic, you're acting the way Sarai did, and it is difficult for your husband to lead you. Keep in mind that God holds him responsible for the leadership of your marriage and family *first*, which can be a burdensome task at times. And He holds you accountable for how cooperative you are in the process.

Through the apostle Paul, God gives these instructions to us as husbands and wives:

> **Out of respect for Christ, be courteously reverent to one another. Wives, understand and support your husbands in ways that show your support for Christ. The husband provides leadership to his wife the way Christ does to his church, not by domineering but by cherishing. So just as the church submits to Christ as he exercises such leadership, wives should likewise submit to their husbands.**
>
> **— Ephesians 5:21-24 (*MSG*)**

The Father and Mother of Faith

When most believers think about the subject of faith, they think of Abraham. He is known in Scripture as *the father of faith*, and Sarah is known as *the mother of faith*. As imperfect as they were, their trust in God was sincere and consistent, growing stronger and stronger all the way to the end of their life. Again and again, the Bible says, "…Abraham believed God, and it was credited to him as righteousness" (Romans 4:5 *NIV*).

There is a very interesting description of Abraham and Sarah that God Himself made in Isaiah 51:1 and 2. He said, "Hearken to me, ye that follow after righteousness, ye that seek the Lord: look unto the rock whence ye are hewn, and to the hole of the pit whence ye are digged. Look unto Abraham your father, and unto Sarah that bare you…."

Basically, God called Abraham a "rock," meaning he was hard, immovable, and difficult to deal with. And Sarah is called a "pit," possibly implying that she was *pit*iful or like a deep, dark, hole in the ground that was difficult to get out of. In any case, neither the rock nor the pit painted a good picture. Yet over time, they humbled themselves before God and learned how to walk together, and they became the father and mother of faith.

The supernatural transformation we see that God did in Abraham and Sarah should give all of us hope for our marriages. If He can change these two rough-around-the-edges individuals and make them the father and mother of faith, He can certainly transform you and your spouse into a trophy of His grace.

How Wives Are To Interact With Their Husbands

To help women grow and become wives that are a blessing to their husbands, Peter wrote to believers and said, "Likewise, ye wives, be in subjection to your own husbands; that, if any obey not the word, they also may without the word be won by the conversation of the wives; While they behold your chaste conversation coupled with fear" (1 Peter 3:1,2).

This same passage in *The Living Bible* says, "Wives, fit in with your husbands' plans; for then if they refuse to listen when you talk to them about the Lord, they will be won by your respectful, pure behavior. Your godly lives will speak to them better than any words."

Peter went on to say, "Don't be concerned about the outward beauty that depends on jewelry, or beautiful clothes, or hair arrangement" (1 Peter 3:3 *TLB*). Although there is nothing wrong with fixing one's hair, wearing nice clothes, and putting on makeup, God doesn't want our temporary, outward appearance to take priority over developing inner godly character that is eternal.

That's what Peter meant when he said, "But let it be the hidden man of the heart, in that which is not corruptible, even the ornament of a meek and quiet spirit, which is in the sight of God of great price" (1 Peter 3:4). The word "meek" here is a Greek word that describes a very strong-willed person who has learned how to bring their soul under control. Equally important is the word "quiet," which would better be translated as *controlled*.

Peter then added, "For after this manner in the old time the holy women also, who trusted in God, adorned themselves, being in subjection unto their own husbands: Even as Sara obeyed Abraham, calling him lord:

whose daughters ye are, as long as ye do well, and are not afraid with any amazement" (1 Peter 3:5,6).

Interestingly, Peter pointed specifically to Sarah and said she "obeyed" Abraham. This word "obeyed" is the Greek word *hupakouo*. It is a compound of the words *hupo*, meaning *under*, and *akouo*, which means *I hear*. When these words are compounded to form the new word *hupakouo*, it means *to come under one's authority and to open the ears to hear and to follow what is being communicated*. Thus, Sarah learned to come under Abraham's authority and open her ears and follow what he communicated to her.

She also learned to call Abraham "lord," which is a translation of the Greek word *kurios*, and it means *lord* or *supreme master*. It took quite a long time, but by the end of Sarah's life, she learned to submit to Abraham's authority as being God's authority in her life.

Trusting in God Is the Key

Ladies, the real key to grasp is that these women of old "trusted in God" (1 Peter 3:5). They weren't looking to or trusting in their husbands. They were looking to and putting their trust *in God*. Even if your husband is messing up, look beyond him to the Lord, and put your trust in Him. You can say, "Lord, I'm trusting You with my husband. I really don't understand many of the things he does, but I choose to trust that You're in control."

Whether you're a man or a woman, this same way of thinking can be applied to anyone who is in authority over you. If you're dealing with a difficult boss, an ungodly government official, or a challenging pastor, the key is getting your eyes off of the person in authority and placing them on God. He is the One in charge of your life, and He is most certainly working all things together for your good!

The story of Abraham and Sarah is an amazing example of a man and woman who grew in God. As a wife, Sarah learned to put aside her complaining, argumentative ways that only led to bitterness and barrenness. Rather than focus on her husband's need to change (which was definitely needed), she focused on her *own* need to change, and she became a more helpful wife that the Lord called His *princess*.

In our next lesson, we'll flip the script and focus on a powerful woman in the Old Testament who used all her gifts and feminine ways for evil and personal gain.

STUDY QUESTIONS

Study to shew thyself approved unto God, a workman that needeth not to be ashamed, rightly dividing the word of truth.
— 2 Timothy 2:15

1. Prior to this lesson, what was your perception of Sarah and Abraham's character? How is this teaching helping you to see them in a more realistic light?

2. Like Sarah and Abraham, there are areas in your character that need to change. As believers, it is vital to realize that God and only God is the one who can change — or sanctify — us. We cannot change ourselves. What do Philippians 1:6; First Thessalonians 5:23,24; and Hebrews 13:20 and 21 say that make this truth clear?

3. Take some time to carefully reflect on God's instructions on marriage in Ephesians 5:21-33 and First Peter 3:1-9. As a husband, describe in your own words what God is asking you to do to love and care for your wife. As a wife, describe in your own words what God is asking you to do to love your husband.

4. Have you fallen short of God's expectations of you? Repent and ask Him to forgive you and give you His grace to truly love your spouse the way He desires.

PRACTICAL APPLICATION

But be ye doers of the word, and not hearers only, deceiving your own selves.
—James 1:22

1. If you are a wife, are you a "Sarai" or a "Sarah"? Does your husband see you as a *complainer* and *fighter* against him — or does he see you as a *princess* and *supporter* in his life?

2. While you think he is hard to trust and to follow, have you ever thought that *you* may be difficult to lead? Be honest: if you were him, would you like leading you? Why or why not?

3. The supernatural transformation we see that God did in Abraham and Sarah should give all of us hope for ourselves and for our marriages. What areas of your life would you like to see God change? Would you like to be more merciful, kind, and forgiving? Would you like to be more peaceful, confident, and decisive? Pray and ask God what you can do to better cooperate with Him to see these changes come about — and for the grace to rest in Him while you wait.

LESSON 4

TOPIC

Jezebel — the Epitome of an Evil Woman

SCRIPTURES

1. **1 Kings 16:31** — And it came to pass, as if it had been a light thing for him to walk in the sins of Jeroboam the son of Nebat, that he took to wife Jezebel the daughter of Ethbaal king of the Zidonians, and went and served Baal, and worshipped him.

2. **2 Kings 9:22,30** — And it came to pass, when Joram saw Jehu, that he said, is it peace, Jehu? And he answered, What peace, so long as the whoredoms of thy mother Jezebel and her witchcrafts are so many? …And when Jehu was come to Jezreel, Jezebel heard of it; and she painted her face, and tired her head, and looked out at a window.

3. **1 Kings 21:25** — But there was none like unto Ahab, which did sell himself to work wickedness in the sight of the Lord, whom Jezebel his wife stirred up.

4. **2 Kings 9:10** — And the dogs shall eat Jezebel in the portion of Jezreel, and there shall be none to bury her….

5. **2 Kings 9:33-37** — And he [Jehu] said, Throw her down. So they threw her down: and some of her blood was sprinkled on the wall, and on the horses: and he trode her under foot. And when he was come in, he did eat and drink, and said, Go, see now this cursed woman, and bury her: for she is a king's daughter. And they went to bury her: but they found no more of her than the skull, and the feet, and the palms

of her hands. Wherefore they came again, and told him. And he said, This is the word of the Lord, which he spake by his servant Elijah the Tishbite, saying, In the portion of Jezreel shall dogs eat the flesh of Jezebel: And the carcase of Jezebel shall be as dung upon the face of the field in the portion of Jezreel; so that they shall not say, This is Jezebel.

6. **Proverbs 6:16-19** — These six things doth the Lord hate: yea, seven are an abomination unto him: A proud look, a lying tongue, and hands that shed innocent blood. An heart that deviseth wicked imaginations, feet that be swift in running to mischief, a false witness that speaketh lies, and he that soweth discord among brethren.

7. **Proverbs 14:1** — Every wise woman buildeth her house: But the foolish plucketh it down with her hands.

8. **Romans 6:13** — Neither yield ye your members as instruments of unrighteousness unto sin: but yield yourselves unto God, as those that are alive from the dead, and your members as instruments of righteousness unto God.

GREEK WORDS
There are no Greek words in this lesson.

SYNOPSIS
So far we have looked at the lives of three powerful women in the Old Testament: Eve, the mother of all the living; Noah's wife, the nameless woman who changed history; and Sarah, the griper and complainer who God radically changed.

Just as women can use their influence to shape their world and the people around them in a positive way, they can also use their influence in negative ways. Few women in Scripture demonstrate a more damaging and destructive impact than the woman named *Jezebel*. Her legacy is so dreadful that no one in their right mind would want to give their daughter or granddaughter that name. Indeed, she is the epitome of an evil woman.

The emphasis of this lesson:

Just as many women in Scripture used their power and influence for good, Jezebel used hers for evil, selfish gain. She manipulated and

controlled others to get her way all through her life and was the embodiment of everything the Lord hates. She was a foolish woman who became a weapon of unrighteousness.

What Do We Know About Jezebel?

Jezebel was no ordinary woman. She was beautiful, sophisticated, and attracted immediate attention everywhere she went — including the attention of a man named Ahab. Ahab was the son of Omri, who served as king of Israel for 12 years and is best known for establishing the city of Samaria. When Omri completed his evil reign, Ahab took his place.

When Ahab laid eyes on Jezebel, he was captivated by her, and the Bible says, "…He took to wife Jezebel the daughter of Ethbaal king of the Zidonians, and went and served Baal, and worshipped him" (1 Kings 16:31). From this passage, we see that Jezebel was the daughter of the king of Zidonians, which is another name for Sidonians, the region of Phoenicia where the Philistines lived. Her marriage to Ahab was politically arranged in order to unify the people of Israel and Phoenicia.

History reveals that Jezebel was a worshiper of Melkart — a form of the god Baal — and the chief god of Phoenicia. When Jezebel became queen of Israel, she brought the worship of Melkart (Baal) with her, and she began promoting Baal worship all over the land. She became notorious for her "whoredoms" and "witchcrafts" (*see* 2 Kings 9:22 and 30).

Not only did Jezebel advocate Baal worship and contaminate the land with idolatry and witchcraft, she also killed many of the prophets of the Lord. Those who escaped her wrath hid within caves — some of which were cared for by the prophet Obadiah (*see* 1 Kings 18:3,4). When the Spirit of God came upon Elijah and he destroyed 450 prophets of Baal, Jezebel threatened to kill him (*see* 1 Kings 19:1,2). She claimed her voice was equal to that of Elijah.

Without question, Jezebel was devious and manipulative. She controlled people like puppets, including Ahab and the whole land of Israel, which she indirectly controlled through her husband's throne. First Kings 21:25 says, "But there was none like unto Ahab, which did sell himself to work wickedness in the sight of the Lord, *whom Jezebel his wife stirred up.*" Day in and day out, this wicked woman incited and manipulated her husband to do whatever she wanted him to do.

This was the character of Jezebel and demonstrates the influence of an ungodly wife.

The Epitome of a Manipulator

A classic example of Jezebel's conniving, manipulative ways is seen in the story of what she did to secure a piece of property that rightfully belonged to someone else. The Bible says, "…Naboth the Jezreelite had a vineyard which was in Jezreel, next to the palace of Ahab king of Samaria. So Ahab spoke to Naboth, saying, 'Give me your vineyard, that I may have it for a vegetable garden, because it is near, next to my house; and for it I will give you a vineyard better than it. Or, if it seems good to you, I will give you its worth in money'" (1 Kings 21:1,2 *NKJV*).

When Naboth rejected the offer, saying he wanted to keep the land in the family and pass it on as an inheritance to his children, Ahab went into depression. Like a spoiled child who couldn't have his way, he went to his room, lay on his bed, and refused to eat.

When Jezebel saw Ahab sulking and sad and learned what had happened, she concocted a scheme to get him the land. Taking plagiarism to a whole new level, she used the king's name and signature seal and began writing letters to the elders of the city, calling them to a ceremonial fast in which two men — identified as the sons of Belial — were manipulated to stand up and falsely accuse Naboth of blaspheming God and the king.

The people believed the false testimony, and Jezebel's scheme went off without a hitch. For Naboth's fabricated crime, she ordered that he be stoned to death. Once it was determined that Naboth was dead, "…Jezebel said to Ahab, Arise, take possession of the vineyard of Naboth the Jezreelite, which he refused to give thee for money: for Naboth is not alive, but dead" (1 Kings 21:15).

This powerful woman used her position, her giftings, and her influence for evil. Ladies, this should serve as a sobering warning to check the motives of your heart for what you're doing and why you're doing it. If your heart — as well as your gifts and talents — are not submitted to the Lordship of Jesus, your actions can become quite destructive. [You can read the full story on Jezebel's actions against Naboth in First Kings 21:1-16.]

Jezebel's Death Was Dreadful

After serving as king of Israel for 22 years, the life of Ahab was snuffed out in battle against the Syrians. God had told Elijah to anoint a man name Jehu to take his place as king. Amazingly, Jezebel attempted to continue ruling the land, this time through her son Joram. But God had already prophesied the death of this wicked woman through the prophet Elijah saying, "And the dogs shall eat Jezebel in the portion of Jezreel, and there shall be none to bury her..." (2 Kings 9:10).

Like a madman on a mission, Joram drove his chariot wildly into Jezreel. "And it came to pass, when Joram saw Jehu, that he said, is it peace, Jehu? And he answered, What peace, so long as the whoredoms of thy mother Jezebel and her witchcrafts are so many? ...And Jehu drew a bow with his full strength, and smote Jehoram between his arms, and the arrow went out at his heart, and he sunk down in his chariot" (2 Kings 9:22,24).

With Jehoram (Joram) out of the way, Jehu turned his attention to Jezebel. The Bible says, "And when Jehu was come to Jezreel, Jezebel heard of it; and she painted her face, and tired her head, and looked out at a window" (2 Kings 9:30). With an air of defiance, Jezebel refused to recognize the duly anointed king. In her mind, she was the ultimate authority. Rather than humble herself and submit to God, she painted her face and in pride looked down at Jehu, attempting to seduce him into a false peace agreement. But Jehu saw right through her arrogance and manipulation.

The Bible says, "And he [Jehu] said, Throw her down. So they threw her down: and some of her blood was sprinkled on the wall, and on the horses: and he trode her under foot. And when he was come in, he did eat and drink, and said, Go, see now this cursed woman, and bury her: for she is a king's daughter. And they went to bury her: but they found no more of her than the skull, and the feet, and the palms of her hands" (2 Kings 9:33-35).

In an instant, the prophecy concerning her death was fulfilled. Second Kings 9:36 and 37 says, "Wherefore they came again, and told him [Jehu]. And he said, This is the word of the Lord, which he spake by his servant Elijah the Tishbite, saying, In the portion of Jezreel shall dogs eat the flesh of Jezebel: And the carcase of Jezebel shall be as dung upon the face of the field in the portion of Jezreel; so that they shall not say, This is Jezebel."

Because she had been devoured by dogs, there would be no grave for the notorious Jezebel. The only memory of her would be the defecation from the animals that would fertilize a nearby field.

Why Did the Dogs Not Eat Her Head, Her Hands, or Her Feet?

Maybe you're wondering why the dogs selectively chose not to eat Jezebel's skull, the palms of her hands, or her feet? To answer this question, we need to turn to the book of Proverbs and read a sobering warning about seven specific things God hates.

> **These six things doth the Lord hate: yea, seven are an abomination unto him: A proud look, a lying tongue, and hands that shed innocent blood, an heart that deviseth wicked imaginations, feet that be swift in running to mischief, a false witness that speaketh lies, and he that soweth discord among brethren.**
>
> **— Proverbs 6:16-19**

A careful study of Jezebel's life reveals that she had committed all seven of these abominations — some of them multiple times. With great arrogance, she operated as a law unto herself, making the rules and breaking the rules as she saw fit. She did whatever she pleased to accomplish her selfish agenda. Her pride and high-mindedness — along with her lying tongue — is what caused the dogs not to eat her *head*.

The dogs didn't eat her *hands* because her hands had shed so much blood. Likewise, the dogs wouldn't eat her *feet* because she was constantly running to mischief. Without a doubt, Jezebel had…

- a proud look
- a lying tongue
- hands that shed innocent blood
- a heart that devised wicked imaginations
- feet that were swift in running to mischief
- a mouth that bore false witness and spoke lies
- a reputation for sowing discord among people

She was an arrogant, conniving, manipulative woman who constantly lied to get her way. She hurt people deeply with her words and actions and interfered in other people's business to ensure that her plans prevailed. She was given to mischief as well as to gossip and making up stories. She was a source of strife that ultimately destroyed her husband, her children, and herself.

God's Word says that women have a powerful choice: "Every wise woman buildeth her house: but the foolish plucketh it down with her hands" (Proverbs 14:1). Jezebel did the latter. In fact, she not only tore down her own home, she also destroyed the nation of Israel by her wicked deeds.

This verse of Scripture can apply to women in a marriage, a family, a church, a business, or a nation. A wise, godly woman will build her marriage, her family, her church, her business, and her nation, while a foolish, ungodly one will tear it down. This is clearly demonstrated in the story of Jezebel. Of course, men have the capability of doing that same thing, which we will see in our series titled *10 Powerful Men*.

What If Jezebel Had Submitted to God?

God had given her many gifts and talents, and she was a strong, strikingly beautiful woman. There is nothing wrong with being a strong woman, but that strength must be submitted to the Holy Spirit's control. Romans 6:13 urges us:

> **Neither yield ye your members as instruments of unrighteousness unto sin: but yield yourselves unto God, as those that are alive from the dead, and your members as instruments of righteousness unto God.**

In the original Greek, the word "instruments," which appears twice in this verse, is actually the word *weapon*. Thus, what we do with all our bodily members and abilities determines what kind of weapon we are — a weapon of righteousness or a weapon of unrighteousness. Jezebel is an example of a weapon of unrighteousness. Indeed, she could have been such a powerful, positive gift to her husband, her sons, and the nation of Israel. Nevertheless, she used her influence and persuasiveness for selfish gain which led to her own destruction.

STUDY QUESTIONS

Study to shew thyself approved unto God, a workman that needeth not to be ashamed, rightly dividing the word of truth.
— 2 Timothy 2:15

1. What new facts and details did you learn about Jezebel (and Ahab) that you did not know?

2. Jezebel's life is inseparably linked with *pride*. Who else in Scripture can you think of whose life was dominated by pride? How did their life end? According to Proverbs 11:2; 13:10; and 16:18, what results from walking in pride?

3. God desires that we live and operate in *humility*. According to James 4:6 and First Peter 5:5, why is humility so vital to us as believers? What are some of the rewards of humility talked about in Psalm 25:9; Proverbs 3:34 and 15:33; James 4:10; and First Peter 5:5 and 6?

PRACTICAL APPLICATION

But be ye doers of the word, and not hearers only, deceiving your own selves.
— James 1:22

1. Are you a strong and influential individual? If so, God made you that way. The question is, have you submitted your gifts, talents, and strengths to the Holy Spirit?

2. Jezebel used her position, her giftings, and her influence for evil and selfish gain. This should serve as a sobering warning to regularly check your heart motives and know *why* you're doing what you're doing. Take a moment to pray and say, *"Lord, please search my heart and reveal my motives. Are my gifts and talents submitted to You? Or am I unknowingly using them for my own selfish purposes?"* Be still and listen. What is the Holy Spirit showing you?

3. Proverbs 14:1 says, "Every wise woman buildeth her house: but the foolish plucketh it down with her hands." When it comes to your marriage, your family, your church, your job, or your business, what do your actions say about your life? Are you wise or foolish?

TOPIC

Bathsheba — the Adulterer Who Became a Godly Example

SCRIPTURES

1. **2 Samuel 11:1-18** — And it came to pass, after the year was expired, at the time when kings go forth to battle, that David sent Joab, and his servants with him, and all Israel; and they destroyed the children of Ammon, and besieged Rabbah. But David tarried still at Jerusalem. And it came to pass in an eveningtide, that David arose from off his bed, and walked upon the roof of the king's house: and from the roof he saw a woman washing herself; and the woman was very beautiful to look upon. And David sent and enquired after the woman. And one said, Is not this Bathsheba, the daughter of Eliam, the wife of Uriah the Hittite? And David sent messengers, and took her; and she came in unto him, and he lay with her; for she was purified from her uncleanness: and she returned unto her house. And the woman conceived, and sent and told David, and said, I am with child. And David sent to Joab, saying, Send me Uriah the Hittite. And Joab sent Uriah to David. And when Uriah was come unto him, David demanded of him how Joab did, and how the people did, and how the war prospered. And David said to Uriah, Go down to thy house, and wash thy feet. And Uriah departed out of the king's house, and there followed him a mess of meat from the king. But Uriah slept at the door of the king's house with all the servants of his lord, and went not down to his house. And when they had told David, saying, Uriah went not down unto his house, David said unto Uriah, Camest thou not from thy journey? why then didst thou not go down unto thine house? And Uriah said unto David, The ark, and Israel, and Judah, abide in tents; and my lord Joab, and the servants of my lord, are encamped in the open fields; shall I then go into mine house, to eat and to drink, and to lie with my wife? as thou livest, and as thy soul liveth, I will not do this thing. And David said to Uriah, Tarry here to day also, and to morrow I will let thee depart. So Uriah abode in Jerusalem that day, and the morrow. And when David had called him, he did eat and

drink before him; and he made him drunk: and at even he went out to lie on his bed with the servants of his lord, but went not down to his house. And it came to pass in the morning, that David wrote a letter to Joab, and sent it by the hand of Uriah. And he wrote in the letter, saying, Set ye Uriah in the forefront of the hottest battle, and retire ye from him, that he may be smitten, and die. And it came to pass, when Joab observed the city, that he assigned Uriah unto a place where he knew that valiant men were. And the men of the city went out, and fought with Joab: and there fell some of the people of the servants of David; and Uriah the Hittite died also. Then Joab sent and told David all the things concerning the war.

2. **2 Samuel 11:24,26,27** — And the shooters shot from off the wall upon thy servants; and some of the king's servants be dead, and thy servant Uriah the Hittite is dead also. ... And when the wife of Uriah heard that Uriah her husband was dead, she mourned for her husband. And when the mourning was past, David sent and fetched her to his house, and she became his wife, and bare him a son. But the thing that David had done displeased the Lord.

3. **2 Samuel 12:1-10,13** — And the Lord sent Nathan unto David. And he came unto him, and said unto him, There were two men in one city; the one rich, and the other poor. The rich man had exceeding many flocks and herds: But the poor man had nothing, save one little ewe lamb, which he had bought and nourished up: and it grew up together with him, and with his children; it did eat of his own meat, and drank of his own cup, and lay in his bosom, and was unto him as a daughter. And there came a traveller unto the rich man, and he spared to take of his own flock and of his own herd, to dress for the wayfaring man that was come unto him; but took the poor man's lamb, and dressed it for the man that was come to him. And David's anger was greatly kindled against the man; and he said to Nathan, As the Lord liveth, the man that hath done this thing shall surely die. And he shall restore the lamb fourfold, because he did this thing, and because he had no pity. And Nathan said to David, Thou art the man. Thus saith the Lord God of Israel, I anointed thee king over Israel, and I delivered thee out of the hand of Saul; And I gave thee thy master's house, and thy master's wives into thy bosom, and gave thee the house of Israel and of Judah; and if that had been too little, I would moreover have given unto thee such and such things. Wherefore hast thou despised the commandment of the Lord, to do evil in

his sight? thou hast killed Uriah the Hittite with the sword, and hast taken his wife to be thy wife, and hast slain him with the sword of the children of Ammon. Now therefore the sword shall never depart from thine house; because thou hast despised me, and hast taken the wife of Uriah the Hittite to be thy wife. ...And David said unto Nathan, I have sinned against the Lord. And Nathan said unto David, The Lord also hath put away thy sin; thou shalt not die.

4. **Psalm 51:1-3** — [*To the chief Musician, A Psalm of David, when Nathan the prophet came unto him, after he had gone in to Bathsheba.*] Have mercy upon me, O God, according to thy lovingkindness: according unto the multitude of thy tender mercies blot out my transgressions. Wash me throughly from mine iniquity, and cleanse me from my sin. For I acknowledge my transgressions: and my sin is ever before me.

5. **Psalm 51:7-17** — Purge me with hyssop, and I shall be clean: wash me, and I shall be whiter than snow. Make me to hear joy and gladness; that the bones which thou hast broken may rejoice. Hide thy face from my sins, and blot out all mine iniquities. Create in me a clean heart, O God; and renew a right spirit within me. Cast me not away from thy presence; and take not thy holy spirit from me. Restore unto me the joy of thy salvation; and uphold me with thy free spirit. Then will I teach transgressors thy ways; and sinners shall be converted unto thee. Deliver me from bloodguiltiness, O God, thou God of my salvation: and my tongue shall sing aloud of thy righteousness. O Lord, open thou my lips; and my mouth shall shew forth thy praise. For thou desirest not sacrifice; else would I give it: thou delightest not in burnt offering. The sacrifices of God are a broken spirit: a broken and a contrite heart, O God, thou wilt not despise.

6. **2 Samuel 12:20,24** — Then David arose from the earth, and washed, and anointed himself, and changed his apparel, and came into the house of the Lord, and worshipped: then he came to his own house; and when he required, they set bread before him, and he did eat. ...And David comforted Bathsheba his wife, and went in unto her....

7. **Proverbs 31:10-12 (*NLT*)** — Who can find a virtuous and capable wife? She is more precious than rubies. Her husband can trust her, and she will greatly enrich his life. She brings him good, not harm, all the days of her life.

8. **Proverbs 31:28-31 (*NLT*)** — Her children stand and bless her. Her husband praises her: "There are many virtuous and capable women in

the world, but you surpass them all!" Charm is deceptive, and beauty does not last; but a woman who fears the Lord will be greatly praised. Reward her for all she has done. Let her deeds publicly declare her praise.

9. **Psalm 32:1** — Blessed is he whose transgression is forgiven, whose sin is covered.

GREEK WORDS

There are no Greek words or definitions in this lesson.

SYNOPSIS

Women play a powerful role in God's plans for humanity. Their influence on the lives of those around them can be truly life-giving or extremely devastating. Those who surrender themselves and their gifts and talents to God for His use leave a legacy of strength and blessing for others.

So far, we've seen how God worked through Eve, Noah's wife, and Sarah to bring about His positive purposes in the earth. In our last lesson, we examined the life of Jezebel, one of the most wicked women in history who used all her charms to advance her selfish schemes and promote the worship of Baal.

Bathsheba is another example of a powerful woman in Scripture. Although she was an adulteress and co-conspirator to her husband's murder, she repented of her sins and experienced God's merciful forgiveness and loving restoration. She grew to become a godly wife and the mother of King Solomon.

The emphasis of this lesson:

Bathsheba was a beautiful woman who willingly committed adultery with King David and then was an accommodating co-conspirator to her husband Uriah's death. Yet through sincere repentance, God forgave her sins and transformed her into a godly wife and mother.

Bathsheba Willingly Came to David

The anatomy of adultery requires the willing participation of two people. No one commits this sin on their own. When King David committed adultery, his willing accomplice was Bathsheba, the wife of Uriah the Hittite. Their story begins in Second Samuel 11:1, which says:

> **And it came to pass, after the year was expired, at the time when kings go forth to battle, that David sent Joab, and his servants with him, and all Israel; and they destroyed the children of Ammon, and besieged Rabbah. But David tarried still at Jerusalem.**

Please note that at the appropriate time for David to fulfill his calling and lead his people in battle against Ammon, he abdicated his position. He was at the wrong place at the wrong time, and he became vulnerable to temptation. Second Samuel 11:2 says:

> **And it came to pass in an eveningtide, that David arose from off his bed, and walked upon the roof of the king's house: and from the roof he saw a woman washing herself; and the woman was very beautiful to look upon.**

Apparently David had been lying around for good part of the day, and when the evening came and he couldn't sleep, he got up and began pacing around on his roof. Many scholars say that Bathsheba deliberately exposed herself at that time of the night because she knew that David would be walking on the roof of his house, and he would see her. Again, it was not just David who committed sin; Bathsheba willingly participated in the act. Second Samuel 11:3 and 4 goes onto say:

> **And David sent and enquired after the woman. And one said, Is not this Bathsheba, the daughter of Eliam, the wife of Uriah the Hittite? And David sent messengers, and took her; and she came in unto him, and he lay with her; for she was purified from her uncleanness: and she returned unto her house.**

Now Uriah the Hittite was one of David's closest associates and a member of his mighty men. Hence, it's very likely he knew exactly who Bathsheba was and had possibly even met her before. Knowing full well that Uriah was not home but on the front lines fighting in battle, he misused his kingly authority and sent some of his men to get Bathsheba. Showing no signs of resistance, she came to David and they slept together.

David *and* Bathsheba Conspired
To Conceal Their Sin

Shortly thereafter, "…the woman conceived, and sent and told David, and said I am with child" (2 Samuel 11:5). Bathsheba knew she was in trouble because by the time Uriah would return home, he was going to discover that she was pregnant, and he would know it was not his child. Frantically, she got word to David, and he began scrambling to cover his tracks, Second Samuel 11:6 and 7 says:

> **And David sent to Joab, saying, Send me Uriah the Hittite. And Joab sent Uriah to David. And when Uriah was come unto him, David demanded of him how Joab did, and how the people did, and how the war prospered.**

Here we see David pretending to be very concerned about what was happening with his friends and how they were doing in the war. But the only thought bombarding his brain was how to conceal the fact that he had just betrayed his loyal friend by committing adultery with his wife. With his palms likely sweating and his heart beating violently in his chest, Second Samuel 11:8 says:

> **And David said to Uriah, Go down to thy house, and wash thy feet. And Uriah departed out of the king's house, and there followed him a mess of meat from the king.**

David intended on sending Uriah home to Bathsheba so he would sleep with her, and then later on when he discovered she was pregnant, he would think that the child was his. But the Scripture says:

> **…Uriah slept at the door of the king's house with all the servants of his lord, and went not down to his house. And when they had told David, saying, Uriah went not down unto his house, David said unto Uriah, Camest thou not from thy journey? why then didst thou not go down unto thine house? And Uriah said unto David, The ark, and Israel, and Judah abides in tents; and my lord Joab, and the servants of my lord are encamped in the open fields; shall I then go into mine house, to eat and to drink, and to lie with my wife? as thou livest, and as thy soul liveth, I will not do this thing.**
> **— 2 Samuel 11:9-11**

Clearly, Uriah was a man of greater integrity than David, who at that point must have been in full-fledged panic mode. After his initial efforts to hide his sin failed miserably, he had to come up with a solid Plan B. Second Samuel 11:12 and 13 says:

> **And David said to Uriah, Tarry here to day also, and to morrow I will let thee depart. So Uriah abode in Jerusalem that day, and the morrow. And when David had called him, he did eat and drink before him; and he made him drunk: and at even he went out to lie on his bed with the servants of his lord, but went not down to his house.**

'Murder, He Wrote'

Once again, David's plan failed. Uriah may have had too much to drink, but his integrity was so strong that even in a state of drunkenness, he would not violate his code of honor. David was quickly running out of options. There seemed to be only one thing left that he could do to hide his infidelity. Second Samuel 11:14 and 15 says:

> **And it came to pass in the morning, that David wrote a letter to Joab, and sent it by the hand of Uriah. And he [David] wrote in the letter, saying, Set ye Uriah in the forefront of the hottest battle, and retire ye from him, that he may be smitten, and die.**

Imagine that! Uriah was sent back to the frontlines of war with his own death warrant in his hand — and he didn't even know it! In David's tormented mind, this was the only remaining route he could take in order to get himself out of the disgraceful trouble he was in. Meanwhile, back at the front, Second Samuel 11:16-18 says:

> **And it came to pass, when Joab observed the city, that he assigned Uriah unto a place where he knew that valiant men were. And the men of the city went out, and fought with Joab: and there fell some of the people of the servants of David; and Uriah the Hittite died also. Then Joab sent and told David all the things concerning the war.**

No matter how you look at it, David killed Uriah, and the blood was not only on *his* hands, but also on the hands of Bathsheba. It is likely that David kept her informed of each thing he attempted to do to conceal their sexual misconduct, including his last-ditch effort to have Uriah "accidentally" killed in battle. The official report from the warfront that came to David included these details:

> **And the shooters shot from off the wall upon thy servants; and some of the king's servants be dead, and thy servant Uriah the Hittite is dead also.**
>
> **— 2 Samuel 11:24**

Thinking his plan had succeeded and that his troubles were over, David breathed a sigh of relief…but it was only temporary. The Bible says, "And when the wife of Uriah heard that Uriah her husband was dead, she mourned for her husband" (2 Samuel 11:26). One can only imagine the myriad of emotions Bathsheba was sorting through in that moment. Certainly guilt and shame seized her soul, along with an ample supply of grief. In her heart, she knew that she was partially responsible for the murder of her husband, who had probably been a very good man to her.

Second Samuel 11:27 informs us, "…When the mourning was past, David sent and fetched her to his house, and she became his wife, and bare him a son. But the thing that David had done displeased the Lord."

Nathan Confronted David of His Sins

About a year after David and Bathsheba committed adultery, a prophet by the name of Nathan who served as God's spokesman in David's life showed up on the scene. Using a cleverly devised tale of two people, he confronted the king about his actions. Second Samuel 12:1-5 says:

> **And the Lord sent Nathan unto David. And he came unto him, and said unto him, There were two men in one city; the one rich, and the other poor.**
>
> **The rich man had exceeding many flocks and herds: But the poor man had nothing, save one little ewe lamb, which he had bought and nourished up: and it grew up together with him, and with his children; it did eat of his own meat, and drank of his own cup, and lay in his bosom, and was unto him as a daughter.**
>
> **And there came a traveller unto the rich man, and he spared to take of his own flock and of his own herd, to dress for the wayfaring man that was come unto him; but took the poor man's lamb, and dressed it for the man that was come to him.**

And David's anger was greatly kindled against the man; and he said to Nathan, As the Lord liveth, the man that hath done this thing shall surely die...

With a covert and stealthy execution, Nathan described the dishonest dealings of David himself. Then in one swift move, he turned to David and said:

...Thou art the man. Thus saith the Lord God of Israel, I anointed thee king over Israel, and I delivered thee out of the hand of Saul;

And I gave thee thy master's house, and thy master's wives into thy bosom, and gave thee the house of Israel and of Judah; and if that had been too little, I would moreover have given unto thee such and such things.

Wherefore hast thou despised the commandment of the Lord, to do evil in his sight? thou hast killed Uriah the Hittite with the sword, and hast taken his wife to be thy wife, and hast slain him with the sword of the children of Ammon.

Now therefore the sword shall never depart from thine house; because thou hast despised me, and hast taken the wife of Uriah the Hittite to be thy wife.

— 2 Samuel 12:7-10

Instantly, the Spirit of God cut straight to the heart of David, convicting him of the grievous sins he had committed. "And David said unto Nathan, I have sinned against the Lord..." (2 Samuel 12:13). David was quick to repent when he was confronted by Nathan the prophet, immediately acknowledging what he had done. Nevertheless, nearly a whole year had elapsed between the crime and the confrontation. Why didn't Nathan confront him sooner? We don't know. Maybe God was waiting to see if David would come forward on his own and confess, or maybe it took Nathan a year to work up the courage to confront David. Whatever the reason, both David and Bathsheba repented of their actions, and out of their experience Psalm 51 was composed.

David's Psalm of Repentance

If there was anyone in Scripture who had a close relationship with God, it was certainly David. When Nathan the prophet came to him and called him out on all of his ungodly actions, his heart was broken, and out of that brokenness he wrote Psalm 51. He began his song of prayer and repentance to God, saying:

> **Have mercy upon me, O God, according to thy lovingkindness: according unto the multitude of thy tender mercies blot out my transgressions. Wash me throughly from mine iniquity, and cleanse me from my sin. For I acknowledge my transgressions: and my sin is ever before me.**
>
> **— Psalm 51:1-3**

David's transgressions included covetousness, stealing, lying, adultery, and murder. What he did to his friend Uriah and the sin that he committed with Bathsheba he would have never tolerated in the lives of those in his service.

And now, after taking and making Bathsheba his wife, every time he looked into her face he was reminded of his thievery, his adultery, his lying, and the murder of his innocent, loyal friend. Indeed, his sin was ever before him. Through the Holy Spirit's conviction, he received correction, he sincerely repented, and he cried out to be cleansed.

> **Purge me with hyssop, and I shall be clean: wash me, and I shall be whiter than snow. Make me to hear joy and gladness; that the bones which thou hast broken may rejoice.**
>
> **— Psalm 51:7,8**

One interesting fact about hyssop is that it was always used in connection with atonement and purification from sin. When the Israelites were being delivered from Egypt, they used hyssop branches to apply the blood of the lamb on the doorposts of their homes. Thus, David's request to be purged with hyssop was his heart's cry for a supernatural cleansing that would be deep and complete.

After describing the brokenness he felt in his life as a result of God's discipline, David went on to say:

> **Hide thy face from my sins, and blot out all mine iniquities. Create in me a clean heart, O God; and renew a right spirit within me. Cast me not away from thy presence; and take not thy holy spirit from me. Restore unto me the joy of thy salvation; and uphold me with thy free spirit. Then will I teach**

transgressors thy ways; and sinners shall be converted unto thee.

— Psalm 51:9-13

Still feeling the enormous weight of grief for his actions, David cried out again for forgiveness, saying, "Deliver me from bloodguiltiness, O God, thou God of my salvation: and my tongue shall sing aloud of thy righteousness. O Lord, open thou my lips; and my mouth shall shew forth thy praise" (Psalm 51:14,15).

Then David revealed one of the most important truths about genuine worship in God's eyes. He said, "For thou desirest not sacrifice; else would I give it: thou delightest not in burnt offering. The sacrifices of God are a broken spirit: a broken and a contrite heart, O God, thou wilt not despise" (Psalm 51:16,17).

Bathsheba Also Repented
and Penned the Words of Proverbs 31

Clearly, David had a broken and a contrite heart over what he had done. This is most apparent in the way he walked through the sickness that took the life of the child born from his adulterous affair. After he had prayed, fasted, and gone many nights without sleep, the child died. And the Bible says, "And David comforted Bathsheba his wife, and went in unto her..." (2 Samuel 12:24).

Bathsheba also repented and confessed her sin to God and experienced His forgiveness. Amazingly, this adulteress and a co-conspirator to murder came clean with the Lord, and she became a godly wife and the mother of Solomon, the man who succeeded David as king and reigned in Israel for 40 years.

What you may not know is that it was Bathsheba who wrote the cherished words of Proverbs 31 describing a godly wife. During Solomon's growing years, she carefully instructed him, saying:

> **Who can find a virtuous and capable wife? She is more precious than rubies. Her husband can trust her, and she will greatly enrich his life. She brings him good, not harm, all the days of her life.**
>
> **— Proverbs 31:10-12 (NLT)**

After listing numerous practical examples of what a godly wife does to provide for her family and generate finances from the works of her hands, Bathsheba added these powerful words:

> **Her children stand and bless her. Her husband praises her: 'There are many virtuous and capable women in the world, but you surpass them all!' Charm is deceptive, and beauty does not last; but a woman who fears the Lord will be greatly praised. Reward her for all she has done. Let her deeds publicly declare her praise.**
>
> **— Proverbs 31:28-31 (*NLT*)**

These words, which women everywhere have continued to read for centuries, were written by Bathsheba — the same woman who committed adultery and collaborated with David to cover their sin by having her husband killed. Her story clearly demonstrates that God can transform the life of anyone who sincerely repents and humbly seeks Him for forgiveness.

Friend, if you've done wrong, don't carry that guilt forever. Take it to the Cross and receive forgiveness. Follow David and Bathsheba's example. They repented, and as a result God blessed them because they had repentant hearts. God will bless your life too, in spite of a bad beginning.

STUDY QUESTIONS

> **Study to shew thyself approved unto God, a workman that needeth not to be ashamed, rightly dividing the word of truth.**
> **— 2 Timothy 2:15**

1. After hearing this fresh retelling of David and Bathsheba's adulterous affair and all that took place as a result, what new insights did you learn — especially about Bathsheba?

2. The Bible says, "For all have sinned, and come short of the glory of God" (Romans 3:23). If you are living and breathing, there are going to be times when you sin. What are you to do when you sin? Read First John 1:7-9 for the answer. (Also consider Proverbs 28:13; 2 Chronicles 7:14; Isaiah 55:7; and Acts 3:19.)

3. Take a few moments to read David's words in Psalm 32 regarding *repentance* and *forgiveness* of sin. What happened to David when he was silent and attempted to hide and ignore his sin? What took place

when he confessed his sins and came clean with God? What warning does he give to those holding onto their sin and refusing to repent?

PRACTICAL APPLICATION

**But be ye doers of the word, and not hearers only,
deceiving your own selves.**
—James 1:22

1. It's crucial to understand that when David should have been leading his men in battle, he chose to take it easy and remain back at his palace (*see* 2 Samuel 11:1). He was at the wrong place at the wrong time and had abandoned what God had called him to do. What does his situation speak to you personally about *your* vulnerability to temptation?

2. Did you start out wrong in your marriage? Were you sexually impure in your relationship? Are you currently involved in inappropriate sexual behavior? If so, there is redemption and restoration for you. If you haven't already repented of your sin and asked God to forgive you, take time to do so now. Consider using David's words of repentance in Psalm 51 and make it a prayer of your own.

LESSON 6

TOPIC

Esther — the Woman Who Saved Her Nation

SCRIPTURES

1. **Esther 2:15,17** (*NKJV*) — Esther obtained favor in the sight of all who saw her.... The king loved Esther more than all the other women, and she obtained grace and favor in his sight more than all the virgins; so he set the royal crown upon her head and made her queen instead of Vashti.

2. **Esther 2:18** (*NKJV*) — ...The king made a great feast, the Feast of Esther, for all his officials and servants; and he proclaimed a holiday in the provinces and gave gifts according to the generosity of a king.

3. **Esther 2:10** (*TLB*) — Esther hadn't told anyone that she was a Jewess, for Mordecai had said not to.

4. **Esther 2:20** (*NLT*) — Esther continued to keep her family background and nationality a secret. She was still following Mordecai's directions, just as she did when she lived in his home.

5. **Esther 4:1** (*NKJV*) — When Mordecai learned all that had happened, he tore his clothes and put on sackcloth and ashes, and went out into the midst of the city. He cried out with a loud and bitter cry.

6. **Esther 5:11** (*TLB*) — All the world knows that anyone, whether man or woman, who goes into the king's inner court without his summons is doomed to die unless the king holds out his golden scepter; and the king has not called for me to come to him in more than a month.

7. **Esther 4:14** (*NKJV*) — …Who knows whether you have come to the kingdom for such a time as this?

8. **Esther 4:16** (*NKJV*) — I will go to the king, which is against the law; and if I perish, I perish!

9. **1 Samuel 1:11** — …O Lord of hosts, if thou wilt indeed look on the affliction of thine handmaid, and remember me, and not forget thine handmaid, but wilt give unto thine handmaid a man child, then I will give him unto the Lord all the days of his life, and there shall no razor come upon his head.

GREEK WORDS

There are no Greek words in this lesson.

SYNOPSIS

When you think about the powerful women in Scripture, the story of Esther more than likely comes to mind. It is a story of great sacrifice, great surrender, and great success for the people of God. This real-life account took place about 479 BC, not long after the Jews were given permission to return to Jerusalem to rebuild the temple. Although there is much we can learn from this woman who saved her nation, let's focus on Esther's great surrender and see what can happen when we choose to hold nothing back from the Lord.

The emphasis of this lesson:

Esther was a powerful woman God raised up and strategically placed within the palace of Medo-Persia at a specific time in history. Although she was young in age, she used her position of influence to save her nation — the nation of Israel — from being exterminated.

Esther's Beginning and Rise to the Top

The setting of Esther's story is the city of Susa, which is located near the Persian Gulf not far from ancient Babylon. At that time Susa was the capital of the Medo-Persian Empire. It had been about 100 years since Nebuchadnezzar first took the Jews into captivity and about 56 years since he was defeated by the king of Persia. It would seem that Esther's parents chose not to return to Jerusalem when King Cyrus granted the Jews the opportunity to do so. However, her mom and dad died when she was very young, and Esther was taken in by her uncle Mordecai who cherished her greatly and raised her in the ways of the Lord.

The Bible reveals that Vashti, the Queen of Persia, refused to come before King Xerxes (also called Ahasuerus) when he summoned her during a week-long banquet. As a result, the king cut her off and banished her from his presence forever. Following the counsel of his advisors, the king then held what we might describe as a "beauty contest." All the beautiful girls throughout the Persian provinces were gathered and brought to the palace in Susa. They each then underwent a series of beauty treatments for 12 months and awaited their special moment when the king would call them.

Of all the girls from which the king had to choose, Esther — the young Jewish maiden — shined brightest in his eyes. The favor of God rested upon her from the moment she entered the palace and was placed in the care of Hegai, the king's eunuch. The Bible says, "…Esther obtained favor in the sight of all who saw her…. The king loved Esther more than all the other women, and she obtained grace and favor in his sight more than all the virgins; so he set the royal crown upon her head and made her queen instead of Vashti" (Esther 2:15,17 *NKJV*).

What's interesting is that when Esther won the beauty contest and was made queen, "…The king made a great feast, the Feast of Esther, for all his officials and servants; and he proclaimed a holiday in the provinces and gave gifts according to the generosity of a king" (Esther 2:18 *NKJV*). Amazingly, the Feast of Esther is still celebrated in Israel today, with people bringing gifts to each other to commemorate the day she was made queen.

She Was an Unlikely Choice

God is always working His plan and His purposes in the world around us — *always*. And the favor on Esther's life was His doing. The fact is, this young Jewish girl who was adopted by her older cousin after her parents had died appeared to be a very unlikely choice to save a nation. Think about it. If you were going to select a person to preserve a group of people from extinction — a nation that would bring forth the Messiah that would save the world — you would probably not select a Jewish girl who won a beauty contest. Yet, that is exactly who Almighty God chose!

To receive this unbelievable honor and walk out this unprecedented assignment, Esther had to give up several things. First, we know she had to give up her name. Originally, she was called Hadassah, but her cousin changed her name to *Esther*, which means *star* and is believed to be connected with Ishtar, the name of the great Babylonian goddess.

Along with giving up her name, Esther also gave up her identity and her culture. The Bible says, "Esther hadn't told anyone that she was a Jewess, for Mordecai had said not to" (Esther 2:10 *TLB*). Even after the king selected her to be queen, "Esther continued to keep her family background and nationality a secret. She was still following Mordecai's directions, just as she did when she lived in his home" (Esther 2:20 *NLT*). Not only was Esther required to surrender her name, her identity, her culture, and even her language, she would also be called upon to surrender her life in order to save her people.

An Evil Plot To Exterminate the Jews

Meanwhile, a major storm was brewing on the other side of the palace. A wicked man by the name of Haman was being honored and promoted by King Xerxes to the position of second in command. In his arrogant mind, no one beside the king was superior to him. Hence, he required that everyone bow before him and show him honor and reverence whenever he came into their presence.

Mordecai, Esther's cousin who conducted business at the king's gate, would not comply with Haman's demands. The only one Mordecai would kneel before was the Lord God, who alone is worthy of worship. Haman became enraged by Mordecai's resistance, and he immediately looked for a way to destroy not only Mordecai, but all the Jews in Persia. You see Haman was an Agagite, whose ancestors were the Amalekites — arch enemies of the Jews that God had commanded the Israelites to completely destroy because of their extremely sinful ways. But the Israelites didn't fully obey God's command (*see* Deuteronomy 25:17-19; Exodus 17:16).

Using his newly acquired position of influence, Haman manipulated and deceived the king into passing a law that would allow for the ultimate destruction of all the Jews. Fueled by intense racial hatred, Haman selected a day — the thirteenth day of the month of Adar (around March) — when all Jews in every province of Persia were to be plundered of their goods and annihilated. The decree was written in the king's name and sealed with the king's signet ring and sent to every province, each in the language of its people.

Mordecai Urged Esther To Plead for the King's Help

The Bible says, "When Mordecai learned all that had happened, he tore his clothes and put on sackcloth and ashes, and went out into the midst of the city. He cried out with a loud and bitter cry" (Esther 4:1 *NKJV*). Then using one of the king's eunuchs, Mordecai got word to Esther about Haman's evil scheme to exterminate the Jews, and he urged her to go before the king and plead for the lives of her people.

To this request Esther replied, "All the world knows that anyone, whether man of woman, who goes into the king's inner court without his summons is doomed to die unless the king holds out his golden scepter; and the king has not called for me to come to him in more than a month" (Esther 5:11 *TLB*).

Mordecai gathered his thoughts and challenged Esther to not be silent but to speak to the king on behalf of the Jews. He then added these most noted words: "...Who knows whether you have come to the kingdom for such a time as this?" (Esther 4:14 *NKJV*) This urgent plea from her cousin, who had raised her as his own daughter, moved Esther to action. She asked Mordecai to gather all the Jews in Susa and to fast for three days and three nights in an appeal to God to grant her favor with the king. She then said, "...I will go to the king, which is against the law; and if I perish, I perish!" (Esther 4:16 *NKJV*)

Of course, we know the end of the story. God gave Esther great favor with King Xerxes, and he permitted her and Mordecai to issue another decree allowing all Jews in every province to defend themselves and avenge themselves on their enemies, which is exactly what they did. God flipped the script, and the Jews successfully destroyed many of their enemies on the very day they themselves were supposed to be destroyed (*see* Esther 8 and 9).

Keep in mind that Esther did *not* know how her story would end. She was walking it out, moment by moment. And she was laying her very life on the line in an attempt to save her people. The depth of character she exhibited was extremely rare. Throughout her life she consistently took the path of humility, humbly respecting and obeying her uncle and all those in authority over her — even submitting to the eunuch Hegai who was in charge of the king's harem. It was her humility before God and others that attracted God's favor and grace and granted her an audience with the king.

The Divine Exchange

In many ways, Esther's story is a great deal like the stories of others in Scripture. Just as she surrendered her life to save her people, others have also willingly surrendered their lives — or the life of the one they held most dear — to receive God's favorable answer to prayer.

Think about Abraham. The Lord had promised him and Sarah a son. Finally, at the age of 100, he received his answer to prayer, and he was blessed with a bouncing baby boy whom he named Isaac. Oh the joy he and Sarah shared as they raised their child of promise, watching him grow and mature into a strong and handsome young man. Then God asked him to do the unthinkable — He asked Abraham to give Him Isaac. When God saw Abraham's willingness to obey and hold nothing back, He stopped Abraham from going through with the sacrifice. He gave Isaac back to Abraham and made him the father of many nations.

Think about Hannah. She was married to a man named Elkanah of the tribe of Ephraim and was unable to have children. Hannah's prayer for a son is a perfect example of what it looks like to surrender something of great value to the Lord in exchange for His favorable answer to prayer.

When the Bible says that Hannah "prayed unto the Lord," it is a vivid picture of the Greek word *proseuchomai*, which is the most frequently used word for "prayer" in the New Testament. It's derived from the word *euche*, which is an old Greek word that describes a *wish*, a *desire*, a *prayer*, or a *vow*. The word *euche* was originally used to depict a person who made a vow to God because of a need or desire in his or her life. This individual would come to an altar and instead of sacrificing an animal, they would *vow* to give something of great value to God in exchange for a favorable answer to prayer.

Hannah made a solemn vow to the Lord, saying, "…O Lord of hosts, if thou wilt indeed look on the affliction of thine handmaid, and remember me, and not forget thine handmaid, but wilt give unto thine handmaid a man child, then I will give him unto the Lord all the days of his life, and there shall no razor come upon his head" (1 Samuel 1:11).

God answered Hannah's request by giving her Samuel, one of the greatest prophets that ever lived. Once Samuel was weaned, Hannah honored her vow and gave him back to God, leaving him to serve and be mentored by Eli the priest. Once Hannah fulfilled her vow, God blessed her with five more sons!

Both Abraham and Hannah's situations are examples of the *divine exchange*. When you sacrificially give something to God, He will always give something back to you, and it will always be bigger, better, and greater than what you gave. God Himself modeled this principle. The Bible says, "For God so loved the world, that he *gave* his only begotten Son…" (John 3:16). What did God receive in return for giving His Son? He received millions upon millions of sons and daughters born into His family through their faith and trust in Jesus Christ!

Live Open-Handed

Esther is a wonderful example for women of all ages everywhere. The thing she is most remembered for is not her extravagant wardrobe or her exquisite jewels or all the pampering she received in the palace. What she is most remembered for and admired for was her willingness to surrender her life and go before the king in order to save her people.

Jesus said, "For whosoever will save his life shall lose it: and whosoever will lose his life for my sake shall find it" (Matthew 16:25). In other words, God wants us to *live open-handed*. He wants us to be willing to give up what we have — even our lives — for Him. And when we do, He will take what we give Him and do something amazing with it!

What has God been talking to you about? Is there a new assignment He's been asking you to say *yes* to? The temptation is often to stay where we're comfortable and with what we are familiar. Esther was probably comfortable with her crown, the palace, and her position in the kingdom. But God wanted to give her a nation. What would have happened had she not been willing to risk her life to go before the king?

We need to be careful not to hold onto what we're familiar with or stay where we are comfortable. If we do, we will likely miss out on the great things God has prepared. The fact is your obedience to what He's calling you to do will have a ripple effect that will positively impact the lives of more people than you could imagine. That's what happened as a result of Esther's obedience.

Be Pliable in God's Hands

Always keep in mind, "…You are not your own… You were bought at a price" (1 Corinthians 6:19,20 *NKJV*). What was that price? The Bible says, "…He paid for you with the precious lifeblood of Christ, the sinless, spotless Lamb of God" (1 Peter 1:19 *TLB*). That is why Paul gives us this holy charge:

> **So here's what I want you to do, God helping you: Take your everyday, ordinary life — your sleeping, eating, going-to-work, and walking-around life — and place it before God as an offering. Embracing what God does for you is the best thing you can do for him. Don't become so well-adjusted to your culture that you fit into it without even thinking. Instead, fix your attention on God. You'll be changed from the inside out. Readily recognize what he wants from you, and quickly respond to it….**
>
> **— Romans 12:1,2 (*MSG*)**

Essentially, this passage is telling us to be attentive to God and live pliable in His hands. That defines a life of surrender. It is the attitude that says, "Lord, You've given me my life and everything in it — my family, my friends, my job, my home, my ministry — *everything*. I have managed it to the best of my ability. It's Yours. I will move where you want me to move and do what You tell me to do. I am Yours to direct. Give me the grace to embrace the place You want and need me to be. In Jesus' name."

STUDY QUESTIONS

1. What new interesting details did you learn about Esther's life? What did she do to get the king's attention and secure his intervention to stop Haman's plan (*see* Esther 5:1-8; 7:1-7)?

2. What was Haman planning to do to Mordecai (*see* Esther 5:9-14)? What ended up happening to Haman (*see* Esther 7:8-10)? What happened to Haman's sons (*see* Esther 9:10)? What does this example speak to you personally about your enemies?

3. How did God instrumentally use Mordecai to save the king's life (*see* Esther 2:19-23)? How was Mordecai honored as a result (*see* Esther 6)? Ultimately, how was Mordecai blessed for his dedicated efforts (*see* Esther 8:1,2; 10:1-3)?

PRACTICAL APPLICATION

1. Have you ever prayed a prayer like Hannah? Have you made a *vow* to give something of great value to God in exchange for His favorable answer to your request? If so, what did you pray, and what did you vow to give God? Did God answer your prayer? Did you honor your vow?

2. What has God been talking to you about? Is there a new assignment He's been asking you to say *yes* to? If so, what do you understand it to be? And what can you do to align yourself with His will and begin to walk out the assignment?

TOPIC

Mary — the Mother of Jesus and the Original Pentecostal

SCRIPTURES

1. **Luke 1:26-38** — And in the sixth month the angel Gabriel was sent from God unto a city of Galilee, named Nazareth, to a virgin espoused to a man whose name was Joseph, of the house of David; and the virgin's name was Mary. And the angel came in unto her, and said, Hail, thou that art highly favoured, the Lord is with thee: blessed art thou among women. And when she saw him, she was troubled at his saying, and cast in her mind what manner of salutation this should be. And the angel said unto her, Fear not, Mary: for thou hast found favour with God. And, behold, thou shalt conceive in thy womb, and bring forth a son, and shalt call his name Jesus. He shall be great, and shall be called the Son of the Highest: and the Lord God shall give unto him the throne of his father David: And he shall reign over the house of Jacob for ever; and of his kingdom there shall be no end. Then said Mary unto the angel, How shall this be, seeing I know not a man? And the angel answered and said unto her, The Holy Ghost shall come upon thee, and the power of the Highest shall overshadow thee: therefore also that holy thing which shall be born of thee shall be called the Son of God. And, behold, thy cousin Elisabeth, she hath also conceived a son in her old age: and this is the sixth month with her, who was called barren. For with God nothing shall be impossible. And Mary said, Behold the handmaid of the Lord; be it unto me according to thy word. And the angel departed from her.

2. **Matthew 1:18** — Now the birth of Jesus Christ was on this wise: When as his mother Mary was espoused to Joseph, before they came together, she was found with child of the Holy Ghost.

3. **Acts 1:12-14** — Then returned they unto Jerusalem from the mount called Olivet, which is from Jerusalem a sabbath day's journey. And when they were come in, they went up into an upper room, where abode both Peter, and James, and John, and Andrew, Philip, and

Thomas, Bartholomew, and Matthew, James the son of Alphaeus, and Simon Zelotes, and Judas the brother of James. These all continued with one accord in prayer and supplication, with the women, and Mary the mother of Jesus, and with his brethren.

4. **Acts 2:1-4** — And when the day of Pentecost was fully come, they were all with one accord in one place. And suddenly there came a sound from heaven as of a rushing mighty wind, and it filled all the house where they were sitting. And there appeared unto them cloven tongues like as of fire, and it sat upon each of them. And they were all filled with the Holy Ghost, and began to speak with other tongues, as the Spirit gave them utterance.

GREEK WORDS

1. "handmaid" — δούλη (*doule*): a female servant
2. "espoused" — μν ηστεύω (*mnesteuo*): originally, to woo and win; to promise in marriage
3. "virgin" — παρθένος (*Parthenos*): a younger woman who is sexually pure, but this word can also be applied to men

SYNOPSIS

When you think about powerful women in the Bible, who comes to mind? We've looked at the lives of Eve, Noah's wife, Sarah, Bathsheba, Jezebel, and Esther, but what about the women of the New Testament? How about Mary, the mother of Jesus? If there is anyone who stands out as important and influential, she is definitely at the top of the list. Indeed, when the angel Gabriel appeared to her to deliver God's assignment, He greeted her by saying, "…Hail, thou art highly favoured [endued with grace], the Lord is with thee: blessed [favored of God] art thou among women!" (Luke 1:28) What can we learn about this special lady that gave birth to and raised the Lord Jesus Christ? What was her home life like when she was growing up? And what was it about her that gave her such great favor with God?

The emphasis of this lesson:

Mary, the mother of Jesus, was a powerful woman who found great favor with God and was chosen to give birth to the long-awaited Messiah. She was with Jesus all through His ministry, at the Cross, and saw

Him after His resurrection. She was also present in the upper room on the day of Pentecost, making her one of the original Pentecostals who received the baptism in the Holy Spirit.

Mary Was Visited by the Angel Gabriel

The most detailed information on Mary and Joseph and the birth of Jesus is found in Luke's Gospel. The Scripture says, "And in the sixth month the angel Gabriel was sent from God unto a city of Galilee, named Nazareth, to a virgin espoused to a man whose name was Joseph, of the house of David; and the virgin's name was Mary. And the angel came in unto her, and said, Hail, thou that art highly favoured, the Lord is with thee: blessed art thou among women. And when she saw him, she was troubled at his saying, and cast in her mind what manner of salutation this should be. And the angel said unto her, Fear not, Mary: for thou hast found favour with God" (Luke 1:26-30).

Isn't that interesting? Twice in these five verses the angel declared that Mary was "favored," which means she had been selected by God for a purpose. The Lord doesn't put everyone's name on small pieces of paper, toss them in a hat, shake them up, reach His hand in and pull one out and say, "Okay, I'll use this person for what I need done." Rather, God chooses specific people for specific purposes.

For what purpose had God specifically chosen Mary? Gabriel said, "And, behold, thou shalt conceive in thy womb, and bring forth a son, and shalt call his name Jesus. He shall be great, and shall be called the Son of the Highest: and the Lord God shall give unto him the throne of his father David: And he shall reign over the house of Jacob for ever; and of his kingdom there shall be no end. Then said Mary unto the angel, How shall this be, seeing I know not a man?" (Luke 1:31-34).

It's important to see that Mary didn't say, "There's no way that can be done. I have never had sexual relations with a man, so what you're saying is impossible." Instead of arguing or doubting that what the heavenly visitor declared would come true, she simply asked with an open heart, "*How* will this be done?"

The Bible says, "And the angel answered and said unto her, The Holy Ghost shall come upon thee, and the power of the Highest shall over-shadow thee: therefore also that holy thing which shall be born of thee shall be called the Son of God. And, behold, thy cousin Elisabeth, she hath also conceived a son in her old age: and this is the sixth month with her, who was called barren. For with God nothing shall be impossible. And Mary said, Behold the handmaid of the Lord; be it unto me according to thy word. And the angel departed from her" (Luke 1:35-38).

Notice the word "handmaid" used here in verse 38. It is the Greek word *doule*, which is from the word *doulos*, and it describes *a female servant* or *slave*. Thus, Mary was basically saying, "I am the Lord's servant — a slave for His purposes. I'm available for whatever assignment you want to give me."

What Was Mary's Life Like While Growing Up?

Along with what the Bible reveals, there are other early Christian writings from the first, second, and third centuries that tell us more about the life of Mary — including the time before she met Joseph. For instance, other early Christian records show that Mary's parents were older and had no children. They prayed for several years asking God to give them a child — even making a vow that if the Lord would give them a child, they would give that child back to the Lord.

Early Christian writers tell us that when Mary was born, her parents presented her to the Lord and dedicated her for God's service. Therefore, from the time she was an infant, the understanding of being dedicated to God was implanted into her heart and mind. "You are not here by accident," her parents likely told her. "You were born into the world to serve God, and He has a special assignment for your life." And she believed what her parents told her.

Without question, Mary's parents raised her in a home where God's Word was a priority, and it shaped her spiritually and made her spiritually sensitive. She was taught to have a pliable heart and to believe she was to obey God. Accordingly, when God revealed His will to her through Gabriel — that she had been chosen to be the mother of the Messiah — she accepted it without deep struggle. She had been purposefully prepared by her parents and taught to serve God faithfully — explicitly obeying whatever He asked her to do.

This shows the importance of dedicating your children — and grand-children — to the Lord. It's never too late to commit your family to the Lord's care and service. There are many churches today that have baby dedications, which are wonderful times of celebration. But if you stop to think about it, a baby dedication is really a *parent dedication*. It is a public ceremony in which parents or guardians bring their children and make a pledge before God and all who are present to raise their kids according to God's Word and His ways.

Mary's life demonstrates how powerful your words and training are in the life of your kids. The Bible says, "Train up a child in the way he should go: and when he is old, he will not depart from it" (Proverbs 22:6). If you haven't done so already, dedicate your children and grandchildren to the care and service of the Lord and begin to instill in their hearts and minds that God has a special purpose for their lives. Then watch in amazement at how God answers your ongoing prayers in remarkable ways!

What We Know About Mary's Father

Early records reveal that Mary's father was in full-time ministry as a *scroll scholar*. Today, we might call him the librarian of the sacred scrolls of the Old Testament. Clearly, his life was built around a commitment to the Scriptures. As a scroll scholar, he was in the synagogue all the time, as that is where the scrolls were kept. Consequently, his family was absorbed in service to the Lord as well. Today, we might say Mary's father was a dedicated, church-going man of the Word. He and his family were in "church" often — which to them was the synagogue — and their lives were built around serving God.

Without question, the Word of God was spoken and talked about on a regular basis in Mary's home. From the time she was born until the day she married Joseph and left home, the Word of God was deposited deep within the soil of her heart, and she was well prepared for her role as the mother of the Messiah.

History reveals that Mary's father and her family relocated to Nazareth at some point in her young life. And while they lived in Nazareth, her father served as the overseer of the sacred scrolls in the synagogue of the nearby town of Sepphoris. It was located just a few miles away, and it was a city of great magnificence and beauty. Again, this shows how Mary's father

— and their family — was dedicated to the Scriptures and serving in the local "church."

Think about your own children and grandchildren. Do you take them to church? Are you building in them a mindset that attending and serving in the local church is *optional* or *essential* to being a Christian? If your attendance and involvement is sporadic, you are indirectly telling them that being a part of the Church is not important and less of a priority than other things. Think of it this way: Do you ask your children or grandchildren if they want to go to school? Of course not. You know they need a quality education, so you make them go to school. And a spiritual education and serving God is even more important.

Please realize that having respect and appreciation for the Church and experiencing the rich blessings it brings will not just happen automatically in your kids' lives. You will have to purposely build it into them. That's what Mary's father and mother cultivated in her life. It was not an accident that Mary became a willing vessel to give birth to and raise the Son of God. She had been nurtured in God's Word and taught to attend God's house and to do God's will. Therefore, when the fullness of time came, she was ready to step into God's will for her life.

What Does It Mean To Be 'Espoused'?

Another important thing to understand about Mary is that she was "espoused" to Joseph. Matthew 1:18 says, "Now the birth of Jesus Christ was on this wise: When as his mother Mary was *espoused* to Joseph, before they came together, she was found with child of the Holy Ghost." The word "espoused" here is a translation of the Greek word *mnesteuo*, which originally meant *to woo and win*. It signified that one was *promised or pledged in marriage*.

In some areas of Scripture, the word "betrothed" is used in place of "espoused." In modern terms, the word "betrothed" would describe an *engagement*. Hence, when Mary was *engaged*, or pledged, to be married to Joseph — *before* the wedding ceremony had taken place and *before* they had come together sexually — she was pregnant with baby Jesus.

In biblical times, Jewish girls were traditionally eligible for "betrothal" as early as the age of 12. It is believed that Mary was between the ages of 12 and 14 when she became "betrothed" or "espoused" to Joseph. At that time, as tradition dictated, a public announcement of their marital intention was made. Joseph and Mary then entered one year of training and preparation for marriage — just like all other engaged couples. The girls learned from the women in the family, and the young men learned from the older men. At the end of that period, there was a ceremony in which the bride and groom were finally joined.

During the one-year preparation time, the couple did not have sex. It was a *full year* of purity and preparation for a life-long commitment. They took marriage very seriously and did not rush into it. One reason marriages fail today is because people are not properly prepared for it. This was not the case with the Jews. They knew marriage was the most important relationship in life, so preparing for it had supreme importance. Marriage is serious and should *not* be rushed into quickly.

Luke 1:27 confirms what Matthew 1:18 says. It states that Mary was "a virgin" and was "espoused" to a man named Joseph. The word "virgin" here is the Greek word *Parthenos*, which describes *a younger woman who is sexually pure*; it can also refer to a man that is sexually pure. And the word "espoused," as we just saw, refers to the Hebrew concept that indicates a man and woman have made a public announcement that they are in the year of preparation and purity. It was during this time of preparation — "before they came together" — "that [Mary] was found with child, of the Holy Ghost" (Matthew 1:18).

Mary Was an Original Pentecostal

So we know from Scripture that Mary gave birth to Jesus, and she and Joseph raised Him in the ways of God (*see* Luke 2). The other specific things we know about Mary are:

- She was at the Cross with Jesus when He was crucified (*see* John 19:25-27).
- She saw him after the resurrection.

AND

- She was in the upper room on the day of Pentecost and spoke in tongues.

Look at what Luke wrote in Acts 1:12-14:

> **Then returned they unto Jerusalem from the mount called Olivet, which is from Jerusalem a sabbath day's journey. And**

when they were come in, they went up into an upper room, where abode both Peter, and James, and John, and Andrew, Philip, and Thomas, Bartholomew, and Matthew, James the son of Alphaeus, and Simon Zelotes, and Judas the brother of James. These all continued with one accord in prayer and supplication, with the women, and Mary the mother of Jesus, and with his brethren.

Take a moment to reread the very last sentence of the passage, paying special attention to the last nine words: "These all continued with one accord in prayer and supplication, with the women, *and Mary the mother of Jesus, and with his brethren.*" It clearly states that Mary the mother of Jesus — and Jesus' brothers — were in the upper room, praying and waiting for the Holy Spirit to come.

This brings us to the day of Pentecost itself, which Luke begins to describe in Acts 2:1-4:

And when the day of Pentecost was fully come, they were all with one accord in one place. And suddenly there came a sound from heaven as of a rushing mighty wind, and it filled all the house where they were sitting. And there appeared unto them cloven tongues like as of fire, and it sat upon each of them. And they were all filled with the Holy Ghost, and began to speak with other tongues, as the Spirit gave them utterance.

Did you catch that? They were *all* filled with the Holy Spirit and began to speak with other tongues. The word *all* means *everyone present* in the upper room — including Mary the mother of Jesus! Thus, Mary was one of the original tongue-talking Pentecostals!

As the disciples preached the Gospel and the Church began to grow, Mary eventually made her way from the land of Israel to the church in Ephesus. If you remember, when Jesus was dying on the Cross, He turned and looked to John and entrusted Mary into his care (*see* John 19:25-27). Years later, when John moved to Ephesus to oversee the church there, Mary went and lived in Ephesus as well until the time of her death. It is most likely that while she was living in Ephesus, she was interviewed by Luke — the physician and historian — and told him all the details of the story of Jesus' birth and upbringing.

A Summary of Mary the Mother of Jesus

Mary was a long-awaited answer to her parents' prayers. Immediately after she was born, her parents dedicated her completely to the service of God. It was instilled in her that she was brought into the world for a divine purpose and that she was to obey God when He revealed His will. The Scriptures were spoken regularly in her home and into her heart by her parents. The lives of Mary and her entire family were built around service to God in His house. By the time the angel Gabriel appeared to her between the ages of 12 and 14 and gave her God's assignment to birth and raise His Son, Mary was ready to believe and receive what the angel said.

Friend, nothing in God's plan is coincidental or accidental — everything is done by God on purpose and for a purpose. Mary was chosen and mightily used by God because she was prepared! What do you believe and understand God is asking you to do to bring Him glory and advance His Kingdom? How are you preparing for it?

STUDY QUESTIONS

Study to shew thyself approved unto God, a workman that needeth not to be ashamed, rightly dividing the word of truth.
— 2 Timothy 2:15

1. As you read through this lesson, what new facts did you learn about Mary, her parents, and her homelife as a child? How does this give you a better appreciation of who she is and why God selected her to be the mother of Jesus?

2. Like Mary, is God asking you to do something that seems impossible? If so, meditate on and hide in your heart His promises to you in Matthew 19:26; Mark 14:36; and Luke 1:37.

3. As you step out in obedience to do what God is asking you to do, consider what He said to Abraham in Genesis 18:14, to Jeremiah in Jeremiah 32:27, and what He spoke through Paul in Ephesians 3:20. How do these passages encourage you and give you hope?

PRACTICAL APPLICATION

But be ye doers of the word, and not hearers only,
deceiving your own selves.
—James 1:22

1. Just after Mary was born, her parents dedicated her completely to the service of God. They raised her to believe she had great purpose and that she was to obey God when He revealed His will. How about you? Have you dedicated your children — and grandchildren — to God? Are you instilling in them the fact that they have a unique purpose, and that God has a special plan for their life? What do you believe and understand God is asking you to do to bring Him glory and advance His Kingdom? How are you preparing for it?

2. Imagine for a moment that you are Mary, and you've been chosen by God to give birth to Jesus, His Son. In light of the fact that you appear to be pregnant out of wedlock, what kinds of personal thoughts and feelings might you have to work through? What types of challenges do you think you might have to sort out initially with Joseph? How about with your family and friends?

3. Interestingly, when God chose to bring His Son into the world, He conceived and produced two babies from two impossible places: Elizabeth's dead womb that was beyond the ability to bear children birthed John; and Mary's virgin womb that had been untouched by a man birthed Jesus. What does this say to you about the character of God? How does it affect your expectations regarding your situation?

LESSON 8

TOPIC

Mary Magdalene — a Woman Who Was Delivered by Jesus

SCRIPTURES

1. **Luke 8:2,3** — And certain women, which had been healed of evil spirits and infirmities, Mary called Magdalene, out of whom went

seven devils, and Joanna the wife of Chuza Herod's steward, and Susanna, and many others, which ministered unto him of their substance.

2. **Mark 16:9** — Now when Jesus was risen early the first day of the week, he appeared first to Mary Magdalene, out of whom he had cast seven devils.

GREEK WORDS

1. "ministered" — **διάκονος** (*diakonos*): a high-level servant; sophisticated and highly trained servants who served the needs of others; a servant whose primary responsibility is to serve food and wait on tables; it is a picture of a waiter or waitress who painstakingly attends to the needs, wishes, and desires of his or her client; servants who professionally pleased clients; a type of serving that was honorable, pleasurable, and done in a fashion that made people being served feel as if they were nobility

2. "substance" — **ὑπαρχόντων** (*huparchonton*): goods, possessions, or property

3. "healed" — **θεραπεύω** (*therapeuo*): therapy; a healing touch that requires corresponding actions; can depict healing due to many treatments

4. "evil spirits" — **πνευμάτων πονηρῶν** (*pneumaton pomeron*): especially important is the use of **πονηρός** (*poneros*): destruction, disaster, harm, or danger; that which is malicious or malignant; something that is foul, vile, hostile, and vicious; includes not only that which is dangerous to the physical body but also to that which is dangerous to the spirit or mind; often used in the Septuagint version of the Old Testament to describe actions that are damaging to a person's testimony and reputation; wicked, unholy, and impure; used to depict animals that are savage, wild, vicious, and dangerous

5. "infirmities" — **ἀσθένεια** (*astheneia*): an all-encompassing term for all types of sickness and disease; depicts those who are weak, sick, broken, or infirmed in body, mind, emotion; it is indicative of infirmities of all types

6. "out of whom went" — **ἐξέρχομαι** (*exerchomai*): a compound of the word **ἐξ** (*ex*) meaning out, as to make an exit, and the word **ἔρχομαι** (*erchomai*) meaning to go; when compounded, the word **ἐξέρχομαι** (*exerchomai*) means to go out, to drive out, or even to escape

7. "devils" — δαιμόνιον (*daimonion*): evil spirits, demons, devils; this word could depict a person deemed insane; in both secular and New Testament writings it depicted those possessed with evil spirits, who suffered spirit-inflicted mental or physical infirmities

8. "cast" — ἐκβάλλω (*ekballo*): to forcibly evict; to throw out; to cast out; to expel; to drive out; to kick out; historically it was used to describe a nation that forcibly removed its enemies out from its borders

SYNOPSIS

Hopefully it's becoming clear: Women are powerful, and they have a great deal of influence on those around them. Like men, women can be a source of great blessing *or* great destruction in the lives of others. The kind of influence they have depends on what God has done in their hearts.

So far in this series we've seen the example of Eve, whose choices and influence affected the entire human race. Then we looked at Noah's wife — the nameless woman who supported her husband and changed human history. Our next example was Sarah, a woman who began as a very unpleasant individual, but God turned into a princess.

Then we saw Jezebel — a strikingly beautiful and talented woman who used her great influence and power to destroy her husband, her sons, and the nation of Israel. Next, we examined the life of Bathsheba, a woman who started out wrong but ended right because of God's mercy and forgiveness. After that, we studied the wonderful example of Queen Esther — the woman who surrendered her life and saved her nation. And then in our last lesson, we learned about the life of Mary the mother of Jesus, who was also an original Pentecostal.

The emphasis of this lesson:

Mary Magdalene was a successful businesswoman from whom Jesus drove out seven evil spirits. With deep gratefulness in her heart, she gave of her finances to support Jesus' ministry and ensure that others would experience the same supernatural healing and restoration of body, soul, and spirit that *she* had.

Although there has been much speculation regarding the character and vocation of Mary Magdalene over the years, what is most important is what the Bible says about her. One of the places she is mentioned is in

Luke 8:2 and 3. Here, Luke wrote, "And certain women, which had been healed of evil spirits and infirmities, Mary called Magdalene, out of whom went seven devils, and Joanna the wife of Chuza Herod's steward, and Susanna, and many others, which ministered unto him of their substance."

What's interesting about this passage is that it describes people who were partners with Jesus in His ministry. As we will see as we unpack the meaning of these verses, these were women who financially gave into Jesus' ministry because they had been powerfully touched and delivered by the work of His hands.

They 'Ministered' Unto Jesus

First, notice Luke said these women "ministered" unto Jesus. This word "ministered" is the Greek word *diakonos*, which is very important. It described *a high-level servant* or *sophisticated and highly trained servants who served the needs of others*. The primary responsibility of these servants was to serve food and wait on tables. The word *diakonos* — translated here as "ministered" — is a picture of a waiter or waitress who painstakingly attends to the needs, wishes, and desires of his or her client. These were servants who professionally pleased clients in a way that was honorable, pleasurable, and done in a fashion that made the people being served feel as if they were nobility.

Without question, these women did what they did with excellence. Jesus had touched their lives and radically changed them. Out of extreme gratitude, they believed it was their God-given assignment to painstakingly attend to the needs, wishes, and desires of Jesus. Their supreme task was to provide what He and His disciples needed to fulfill their ministry without hindrance. Furthermore, the tense used in the original Greek indisputably means that these women did this task *consistently* and *regularly*. In other words, they habitually donated money to Jesus' ministry and became faithful partners on whom Jesus could rely. Serving the needs of Jesus with excellence and an attitude of gratitude is what we are all called to do.

They Gave of Their 'Substance'

How did these women give? Luke said "of their substance." The word "substance" is a translation of the Greek word *huparchonton*, which describes *goods, possessions, or property*. This word would only be used to describe individuals of great wealth who possessed large fortunes or enormous assets. It lets us know that these were wealthy women.

In the *King James Version*, it says these women ministered unto him *of* their substance, but in the original Greek, it actually says *out* of their substance. This implies that these very wealthy women may have donated funds out of the income they earned on properties they owned or the investments they had made. It was out of their surplus that they sowed generously into Jesus' ministry.

Jesus Had 'Healed' Them

Who were these women who gave into Jesus' ministry? The Bible says they were, "…certain women, which had been healed of evil spirits and infirmities…" (Luke 8:2). Notice the word "healed." There are a few different words in Greek that Luke could have chosen to use here. In this verse, he selected the Greek word *therapeuo*, which basically means *therapy*. It's where we get the word *therapy*, and it describes *a healing touch that requires corresponding actions*.

Interestingly, the word *therapeuo* — translated here as "healed" — can depict *healing due to many treatments*. Just like a person goes through physical therapy and receives treatment again and again and again, the word *therapeuo* suggests that these women had been so severely demonized that although they were helped when they first came to Jesus, they had to keep coming back again and again until finally, they were completely freed.

It's important for you to understand that sometimes for you to experience a full healing and deliverance, it requires many touches of God's power upon your life. Just as Jesus literally therapied these women, He will therapy you as often as you come to Him. He will touch you again and again and again, as much as you need, until finally you are completely delivered.

He Set Them Free
From 'Evil Spirits' and 'Infirmities'

Luke specifically says these women were healed of "evil spirits and infirmities" (Luke 8:2). The phrase "evil spirits" is a translation of the Greek words *pneumaton pomeron*. It is taken from the word *poneros*, which describes *destruction, disaster, harm, or danger*. It is something that is *malicious* or *malignant*; something that is *foul, vile, hostile*, and *vicious*. It includes not only that which is dangerous to the physical body but also that which is dangerous to the spirit or mind.

This word *poneros* — translated as "evil" in this verse — is often used in the Septuagint version of the Old Testament to describe *actions that are damaging to a person's testimony and reputation.* It depicts behavior that is wicked, unholy, and impure. This word was even used to depict animals that are savage, wild, vicious, and dangerous. So when the Bible says Jesus "healed" — or therapied — these women of evil spirits, it means He touched them again and again, delivering their lives from *malicious, foul, vile, hostile, wild, vicious,* and *dangerous demonic forces that were ravaging their lives.* He ministered to them repeatedly until every layer of demonic control was peeled off of their lives and they were set free.

Luke also noted that Jesus healed these women of "infirmities," which is the Greek word *astheneia,* an all-encompassing term for all types of *sickness* and *disease.* Specifically, it depicts those who are weak, sick, and broken, or infirmed in body, mind, or emotion. It is indicative of infirmities of all types. Again, Jesus "healed" (*therapeuo*) them of these sicknesses and diseases, which implies that these women made recurring visits to Jesus before they found total relief from their physical maladies.

Friend, if God has touched you but you don't feel you're totally free yet, keep coming to Him again and again. Sometimes the healing He releases is a therapeutic work of God's power that will require multiple touches over a period of time until you are totally liberated and changed.

It's no wonder that these women were such avid financial partners with Jesus' ministry! It was through His compassionate touch that they were set free from extremely vile and hostile demons and restored to full health! The fact is the best partners in ministry are those whose lives have been changed most drastically by the power of God. These women are vivid examples of people with grateful hearts who want to do whatever they can financially so the ministry that helped them can reach out and touch others' lives as well.

Was Mary Magdalene Once a Prostitute?

Of all the people that Jesus healed in every town and village, Mary called Magdalene is listed by name. Why is she called Magdalene? Good question. Magdalene was not her last name. It refers to Magdala — the place on the coast of the Sea of Galilee near Tiberias from where she came. People from Magdala were called Magdalenes. Hence, Mary was the woman from Magdala.

Over the centuries, many tales have been told about Mary Magdalene, but most of them have no basis in Scripture. For instance, you may have heard she worked in the prostitution business before she met Jesus. In 591 AD, Pope Gregory the Great inferred that she was a prostitute in one of his well-known messages leading up to Easter. However, there is no evidence of this claim in the Bible.

Unfortunately, the idea of Mary Magdalene being a prostitute caught on and was passed on for centuries. It wasn't until 1969 — nearly 1,400 years later — that the Catholic Church admitted the Bible does not support that interpretation. Actually, there isn't a single New Testament verse — or any other source — that says Mary Magdalene was a former prostitute.

Jesus Evicted Seven Devils Out of Mary Magdalene

One thing is clear, though: She was possessed with an infestation of demons before Jesus delivered her. Luke identified her as "…Mary called Magdalene, out of whom went seven devils" (Luke 8:2). Notice the phrase "out of whom went." It is a translation of the Greek word *exerchomai*, which is a compound of the word *ex*, meaning *out*, as to *make an exit*; and the word *erchomai*, meaning *to go*. When these words are compounded, the word *exerchomai* means *to go out*, *to drive out*, or even *to escape*.

It may be that these demons were so entrenched in Mary that Jesus had to literally drive them out of her. When these seven foul spirits finally made their exit out of her body, it is possible that they literally fled in order to escape the fierce pressure Jesus was exercising on them. Once they were gone, Mary was freed.

This brings us to the word "devils," which is the Greek word *daimonion*. It describes *evil spirits, demons,* or *devils*. This word could also describe a person deemed insane. In both secular and New Testament writings, it depicted those possessed with evil spirits, who suffered spirit-inflicted mental or physical infirmities. This implies that when Jesus first met Mary, she may have had mental problems.

The fact that Jesus delivered Mary of seven demonic spirits is confirmed in Mark 16:9, which states, "Now when Jesus was risen early the first day of the week, he appeared first to Mary Magdalene, out of whom he had cast seven devils." The word "cast" in this passage is the Greek word *ekballo*. It is a compound of the word *ek*, meaning *out*, and the word *ballo*, which means *to throw*. When these words are joined to form *ekballo*, it means *to forcibly evict*; *to throw out*; *to cast out*; *to expel*; *to drive out*; *to kick out*; or *to cast out*. Historically, this word was used to describe a nation that forcibly removed its enemies out from its borders.

What Else Does the Bible Say About Mary Magdalene?

Although the Bible does not provide a detailed account of Mary's deliverance from these seven demons, it does let us know that Jesus did cast them out of her, and she was so thankful for what He had done that she remained committed to Him to the very end of His ministry.

Scripture indicates that Mary Magdalene…

- Was often present with the apostles.
- Was present at the crucifixion (John 19:25).
- Was present after the crucifixion when Jesus' body was being prepared for burial. (Mary was among those who prepared His body for burial according to Matthew 27:61; Mark 15:47; Luke 23:55.)
- Was among the first to see Jesus' empty tomb (John 20:1).
- Was the first to see Jesus after His resurrection (John 20:1,13-17).
- Was the first to preach that Jesus had been resurrected from the dead (John 20:18).

We rightly focus on Jesus and the great works He did while on earth. At the same time, think of the reward that is laid up in Heaven for people like Mary Magdalene. She was a powerful woman who used her finances and her influence so others could be helped by Jesus' ministry. Just as she was touched regularly and consistently by the therapeutic power of God until she was totally set free, she helped fund Jesus' ministry with her substance so that other people could experience His therapeutic healing and deliverance.

Mary — and all the others who gave of their substance so that those life-changing meetings could take place — were Jesus' ministry partners. And in Heaven, they all share in the rewards for the results reaped by Jesus' ministry.

If your life has been touched and changed by a specific ministry, it is right for you to desire to give to that ministry to show your gratefulness and to make sure others receive the same touch you received. So when God calls you to be a ministry partner, never forget that what you do is vitally important. The gifts you give from your personal income and assets can make an eternal difference in other people's lives.

STUDY QUESTIONS

Study to shew thyself approved unto God, a workman that needeth not to be ashamed, rightly dividing the word of truth.
— 2 Timothy 2:15

1. What fresh insights about Mary Magdalene has the Holy Spirit given you in this lesson? What did you learn about her life *prior* to meeting Jesus? What did you discover about how she was delivered from evil spirits?

2. Giving money to support ministries has often been controversial in some people's minds. But is it biblical? Examine Paul's candid words in First Corinthians 9:3-14 and Galatians 6:6. What does God's Word have to say about supporting ministries. (Also consider Romans 15:25-27.) How do these passages of Scripture expand your understanding of giving?

3. Sometimes the healing God releases is a *therapeutic* work of His power that requires multiple exposures over a period of time until you are totally liberated and changed. If God has touched you but you don't feel you're totally free or healed yet, keep coming to Him again and again until your healing and restoration is complete. (Consider Jesus' words in Matthew 7:7-11 and Luke 18:1-8.)

PRACTICAL APPLICATION

But be ye doers of the word, and not hearers only, deceiving your own selves.
— James 1:22

1. The word *diakonos* — which is often translated as "minister" in the New Testament — describes a servant who professionally pleases his clients in a way that is honorable, pleasurable, and done in a fashion that makes people being served feel as if they were nobility. Who do

you know that has "ministered" to you in this way? What is it about the way they serve that touches you so deeply? Looking at your own life, would you call yourself a *diakonos* (minister)? Why or why not?

2. The best partners in ministry are those whose lives have been changed most drastically by the power of God. What ministry has God used in your life to bring healing and transformation? Has God asked you to support this ministry with your finances and prayers? If so, have you been obedient? Never forget that what you do is vitally important. The gifts you give make an eternal difference in the lives of others.

TOPIC

Mary — a Woman Who Gave Her Living Room to Jesus

SCRIPTURES

1. **Acts 1:13** — And when they were come in, they went up into an upper room....

2. **Acts 12:12** — And when he had considered the thing, he came to the house of Mary the mother of John, whose surname was Mark; where many were gathered together praying.

3. **John 20:22** — And when he had said this, he breathed on them, and saith unto them, Receive ye the Holy Ghost.

4. **Acts 1:4,5** — And, being assembled together with them, commanded them that they should not depart from Jerusalem, but wait for the promise of the Father, which, saith he, ye have heard of me. For John truly baptized with water; but ye shall be baptized with the Holy Ghost not many days hence.

5. **Acts 4:31** — And when they had prayed, the place was shaken where they were assembled together....

GREEK WORDS

1. "upper room" ὑπερῷον (*huperoon*): the highest part of the house; the upper rooms or upper story of a house; usually the largest open space in an ancient home

SYNOPSIS

Throughout our study on powerful women, we have learned about two ladies named Mary. In Lesson 7, we looked at Mary the Mother of Jesus, and in our last program, we examined the life of Mary Magdalene, a woman who had an infestation of seven demon spirits. It seems those evil spirits were so entrenched inside of her that when she came to Jesus, He had to forcibly drive them out, using the therapeutic power of God. Out of great gratitude for His transforming touch on her life, she began supporting Jesus' ministry financially and using her influence to help others experience His healing power just as she had.

Interestingly, there is yet another Mary who played a powerful role in Jesus' ministry and the development of the Church. It appears that this Mary began following Christ at some point earlier in His ministry, and out of great appreciation for Him, she opened her home to Him and His disciples. As a result, her living room literally became ground zero for some of the greatest events in history. In fact, this room in the city of Jerusalem is so important it has been included in more than 260 verses of the New Testament! What's the name of this notable place? It's called the *Upper Room*, and it is where we are going to spend the entirety of this lesson.

The emphasis of this lesson:

Mary, the mother of John Mark and sister of Barnabas, was a wealthy widow who owned a prestigious house near the temple in Jerusalem. With a desire to honor and support Jesus, she willingly opened her home to Him and His disciples, and it became the epicenter of activity that launched the Gospel and the Church all around the world.

The Upper Room — also known as the "Cenacle," which is the Latin word for *upper room* — was not a public building. It was actually part of a private home, and it can still be visited in Jerusalem today. Since the Fourth Century, this room has been recognized as the historic location where Jesus met regularly with His disciples and where the disciples met regularly with the Holy Spirit and each other for many years after the Church was launched.

It is mentioned specifically in Acts 1:13, which says, "And when they were come in, they went up into an upper room…." The Greek word here for "upper room" is *huperoon*, and it describes *the highest part of the house; the upper rooms* or *upper story of a house*. In an ancient home, it was usually the largest open space. In this case, the upper room was the upper chamber in Mary's home located on the second or third floor. Rooms like these were common in the First Century and served as the first churches.

How do we know the Upper Room belonged to Mary? Because it is identified in the book of Acts. When Peter was released from prison by an angel, he knew where to find the believers. Acts 12:12 says, "And when he [Peter] had considered the thing, he came to the house of Mary the mother of John, whose surname was Mark; where many were gathered together praying." Mary appears to have been a wealthy widow who owned a very large and prestigious house in the center of the ancient city of Jerusalem near the temple. She was the sister of Barnabas, the friend and ministry partner of the apostle Paul throughout his first missionary journey. She was also the mother of John Mark — the same John Mark who eventually moved to Rome and became the secretary to the apostle Peter. John Mark took dictation from Peter and wrote down his account of Jesus' life and ministry. It's what we know today as the gospel of Mark.

When Mary gave her upper room to Jesus, she had no idea that God would use it for more than 2,000 years. Instead of drawing into herself after the loss of her husband and feeling that her life was over, she surrendered what she had to Jesus and opened the doors of her home to Him and His disciples, and as a result history was made — in her home!

THE UPPER ROOM IS WHERE…

Jesus served the disciples Communion (John 13).

On the final night Christ was with His disciples, He ate the Passover meal — also known as the Last Supper — and then served them what we now know as Communion. Although the details of these events are recorded primarily in the synoptic gospels (Matthew, Mark, and Luke), the apostle

John also mentioned this major event in the thirteenth chapter of his gospel. This took place in the Upper Room.

Jesus washed the feet of the disciples (John 13:1-17).

After the Passover meal was ended, the Bible says that Christ laid aside His garments, girded Himself with a servant's towel, and washed His disciples' feet — even the feet of Judas Iscariot, the one who betrayed Him. It may be that Mary assisted Jesus with the preparation of the water basin as He washed each man's feet. This event took place in her Upper Room.

Jesus taught about the Holy Spirit (John 14-16).

After washing the disciples' feet and predicting His betrayal, Jesus said He would be returning to the Father but that He would be sending the Holy Spirit in His place to live inside each believer. He then described the wonderful ministry of the Spirit, including the Spirit's ability to lead us and guide us into all truth and reveal future events yet to come. Christ's teaching on the Holy Spirit recorded in three chapters of John's gospel took place in Mary's Upper Room.

Jesus prayed His high priestly prayer (John 17).

Just before Christ and His disciples made their way into the Garden of Gethsemane, He took time to pray a priestly prayer over His disciples that were with Him and all those who would believe in Him through their witness. Again and again, He asked the Father to unite all of us as one, just as He and the Father are one. This priestly prayer was prayed in the Upper Room.

Jesus appeared to the disciples after His resurrection (John 20:19-31).

After Christ was crucified and placed in the tomb of Joseph of Arimathea, the disciples shut themselves in behind locked doors for fear of the Jews. And while they were in hiding, Jesus suddenly came and stood in their midst and revealed Himself to them. It was at that time that He breathed on them and said, "…Receive ye the Holy Ghost" (John 20:22). Not once, but twice He appeared to them behind closed doors, and this took place in the Upper Room of Mary's home.

Jesus' disciples gathered after the ascension (Acts 1:9-13).

As the disciples stood on the Mount of Olives, they watched Jesus ascend out of their sight into Heaven. Instantly, two angels appeared and comforted them with the news that Christ would one day return again in like manner. The faithful followers of Jesus then returned to the city of Jerusalem and made their way back to their familiar hangout of the Upper Room where they continued to pray and seek God.

Jesus sent the 120 to wait for the promise of the Father (Acts 1:4,5).

As a part of His final words to His disciples, the Bible says Jesus "…commanded them that they should not depart from Jerusalem, but wait for the promise of the Father, which, saith he, ye have heard of me. For John truly baptized with water; but ye shall be baptized with the Holy Ghost not many days hence" (Acts 1:4,5). This commandment was so important it is also recorded in Luke 24:49. Can you guess where the disciples gathered in Jerusalem? Yes, it was in the Upper Room that belonged to Mary.

Matthias was chosen to be an apostle (Acts 1:15-26).

As the disciples and followers of Christ faithfully waited in Jerusalem for the promise of the Holy Spirit, the disciples discussed the need to fill the place vacated by Judas the betrayer. Two individuals who had been with Jesus since the day of His baptism were considered. After a time of prayer, Matthias was selected to fill the position and be counted with the 11 other apostles. This, too, took place in the Upper Room.

The Holy Spirit descended on the Day of Pentecost (Acts 2:1-4).

Fifty days after Jesus had risen from the grave, the promised gift of the Holy Spirit was poured out on the 120 faithful followers who were obediently waiting in the city of Jerusalem. Instantly, they were all filled with the same Spirit that raised Christ from the dead, and they began to powerfully proclaim in the native tongues of the earth the wonderful works of God. The world would never be the same again — and this took place in the same Upper Room of Mary's home.

The house was physically shaken by the power of God (Act 4:23-31).

Evidently, the Upper Room became one of the first places where the Church congregated after the Day of Pentecost. For instance, after Peter and John were arrested and interrogated by the Jewish leaders and then released, they joined the rest of the believers who were already assembled for a time of prayer in the Upper Room of Mary's house. The Bible says, "And when they had prayed, the place was shaken where they were assembled together..." (Acts 4:31).

Peter went when he was released from prison (Acts 12:12-17).

After Herod had Peter arrested and imprisoned, the Church prayed without ceasing for him to be released (*see* Acts 12:5). God heard and answered their prayers by sending His angel to set Peter free. After being led out of prison, Peter fully came to his senses and immediately made his way to the Upper Room in Jerusalem where he knew the saints would be gathered in prayer.

Mary's Home Became an Epicenter of God's Power!

All these magnificent events took place in the same space — the Upper Room of Mary's house. Again, this chamber was located on the second or third floor of her large and prestigious home, which was near the temple in the city of Jerusalem. Mary was the sister of Barnabas and the mother of John Mark, which would make Barnabas John Mark's uncle. The apostle Paul mentioned this family connection in Colossians 4:10, saying, "Aristarchus my fellowprisoner saluteth you, and Marcus, sister's son to Barnabas...." In Greek, the phrase "sister's son" is *anepsios*, which means *nephew* or possibly *cousin*.

Initially, Barnabas took his nephew John Mark with him on Paul's first missionary journey. But because John Mark abandoned them in the city of Pamphylia, Paul didn't want to take him on his second missionary journey. Over time, John Mark matured, and after several years, Scripture informs us that he became Peter's spiritual son and apprentice (*see* 1 Peter 5:13

NKJV). Eventually, John Mark would pen Peter's gospel, which would bear the name "the Gospel of Mark."

Keep in mind it was Mary, John Mark's mom, that was instrumental in this young man's spiritual growth. We know that she loved Jesus, and while she wasn't a prophet or a teacher or a theologian, she was an affluent widow who wanted her son to be exposed to Jesus' ministry and His ministry team. Therefore, she opened her home to them and used her gift of hospitality to take care of the Lord and His disciples, making them feel welcome whenever they were in town. Her home is what was in her hand, and when she surrendered it to Jesus, it became an epicenter from which the power of God could radiate. Amazingly, the Holy Spirit is still ministering to and filling people in the Upper Room today!

STUDY QUESTIONS

Study to shew thyself approved unto God, a workman that needeth not to be ashamed, rightly dividing the word of truth.
— 2 Timothy 2:15

1. Did you know that the Upper Room in Jerusalem was actually owned by Mary? What new facts about this woman of God did you discover in this lesson? What did you learn about the Upper Room? Name the events that you did not know took place in the Upper Room.

2. Clearly, Mary loved Jesus and freely opened the doors of her home to Him and His disciples. What has God promised will happen when you welcome Jesus into your home and life? (Consider Revelation 3:20; James 4:8; Psalm 16:8; 145:18; Matthew 11:28-30.)

PRACTICAL APPLICATION

But be ye doers of the word, and not hearers only, deceiving your own selves.
—James 1:22

1. Imagine you are Mary, and Jesus and His disciples are coming to *your* home and spending time with you and your family regularly. What do you think would make Jesus feel welcome and comfortable in your house? What do you think your life would be like? How do you think your family would be impacted by the presence of Jesus and His disciples?

2. For David, it was a slingshot and five smooth stones. For Moses, it was his shepherd's staff. For Mary, it was her upper room. What's in *your* hand? What has God entrusted to you that you can surrender to Him to help others come to know Him in a more real and personal way? When the power of God attaches itself to our little, it becomes much!

3. Would Jesus feel welcomed and at ease coming in and staying with you? Is there anything present or taking place in your home that you feel would deter Him from entering and taking up residence? If so, what is it? What steps can you take to remove this hindrance of the presence of God in your home? Take time now to invite Jesus to begin working in your life and home.

LESSON 10

TOPIC

Priscilla — a Woman Preacher

SCRIPTURES

1. **Acts 18:1,2** — After these things Paul departed from Athens, and came to Corinth; and found a certain Jew named Aquila, born in Pontus, lately come from Italy, with his wife Priscilla; (because that Claudius had commanded all Jews to depart from Rome:) and came unto them.

2. **Colossians 3:11** — Where there is neither Greek nor Jew, circumcision nor uncircumcision, Barbarian, Scythian, bond nor free: but Christ is all, and in all.

3. **Galatians 3:28** — There is neither Jew nor Greek, there is neither bond nor free, there is neither male nor female: for ye are all one in Christ Jesus.

4. **1 Corinthians 14:34,35** — Let your women keep silence in the churches: for it is not permitted unto them to speak; but they are commanded to be under obedience, as also saith the law. And if they will learn any thing, let them ask their husbands at home: for it is a shame for women to speak in the church.

5. **1 Timothy 2:11,12** — Let the woman learn in silence with all subjection. But I suffer not a woman to teach, nor to usurp authority over the man, but to be in silence.

6. **Romans 16:1** — I commend unto you Phebe our sister, which is a servant of the church which is at Cenchrea.

7. **Romans 16:3-5** — Greet Priscilla and Aquila my helpers in Christ Jesus: Who have for my life laid down their own necks: unto whom not only I give thanks, but also all the churches of the Gentiles. Likewise greet the church that is in their house....

8. **Romans 16:7** — Salute Andronicus and Junia, my kinsmen, and my fellow-prisoners, who are of note among the apostles, who also were in Christ before me.

9. **Romans 16:12** — Salute Tryphena and Tryphosa, who labour in the Lord....

10. **Romans 16:15** — Salute Philologus, and Julia, Nereus, and his sister, and Olympas, and all the saints which are with them.

11. **Romans 8:28** — And we know that all things work together for good to them that love God, to them who are the called according to his purpose.

GREEK WORDS

1. "found" — **εὑρίσκω** (*heurisko*): carries an element of surprise; literally means "I found it"; where we get our word "eureka"

2. "silence" — **σιγάω** (*sigao*): depicts a modification of behavior; in this case, silence or keeping control of one's mouth, as opposed to rambunctious speaking

3. "And if they will learn any thing" — **εἰ δέ τι μαθεῖν θέλουσιν** (*ei de ti mathein thelousin*): if, however, they are really longing to seriously learn

4. "ask" — **ἐπερωτάω** (*eperotao*): interrogate; freely ask; depicts an open conversation

5. "to speak" — **λαλεῖν** (*lalein*): to talk, to converse, to carry on a conversation

6. "learn" — **μανθάνω** (*manthano*): depicts a learner; a disciple; a follower; an apprentice

7. "silence" — **ἡσυχία** (*hesuchia*): does not mean speechlessness, but depicts a calm, as opposed to an inappropriate or unacceptable, behavior

8. "usurp authority" — αὐθεντέω *(authenteo)*: a domineering attitude; to use one's position to take up arms against another; to act as an autocrat; pictures one who with his own hand kills others; to use one's position to dominate or to manipulate

9. "man" — ἀνδρός *(andros)*: man, but here, most likely husband

10. "servant" — διάκονον *(diakonon)*: a female deacon; a servant with delegated responsibilities that often included public and managerial functions

11. "helpers" — συνεργός *(sunergos)*: fellow workers; co-workers; associates; partners

SYNOPSIS

In our first nine lessons, we have focused on the lives of nine powerful women in Scripture. Those included were:

- Eve — the Mother of the Human Race
- Noah's wife — the Nameless Woman Who Changed History
- Sarah — the Woman God Radically Changed
- Jezebel — the Epitome of an Evil Woman
- Bathsheba — the Adulterer Who Became a Godly Example
- Esther — the Woman Who Saved Her Nation
- Mary — the Mother of Jesus and the Original Pentecostal
- Mary Magdalene — a Woman Who Was Delivered by Jesus
- Mary — a Woman Who Gave Her Living Room to Jesus

The last woman we want to take time to look at is a lady by the name of Priscilla. She became a powerful woman preacher who faithfully served in fulltime ministry alongside her husband Aquila and the apostle Paul.

The emphasis of this lesson:

Priscilla and her husband, Aquila, met and joined forces with Paul in the city of Corinth and served together in ministry for many years. Like Priscilla, many women assisted Paul in building the Church, clearly demonstrating that he was for women, not against them, and in Christ all distinctions disappear — including gender.

Aquila and Priscilla Had Been Evicted From Rome

Shortly before — or perhaps at the same time — the apostle Paul arrived in Corinth, Aquila and Priscilla also entered the ancient port city for the first time. This husband-and-wife team had just experienced a very discouraging ordeal themselves, having been ordered to leave their home in the city of Rome. The Emperor Claudius had recently issued an edict to expel Jews from Rome — an imperial decree that especially impacted Jewish believers.

One early Roman historian named Suetonius wrote that Claudius was upset with Jews who "were constantly inciting tumults under their leader Christos." Many historians believe the edict was a reaction in the Jewish community against the rising influence of Jewish Christians who were preaching Christ. It was a sudden, tragic turn of events when Aquila and Priscilla and others were forcefully ejected from their home because of religious persecution.

We're not sure how the event unfolded, but this type of imperial edict was often carried out in an abrupt and harsh manner during early New Testament times. It's very possible that the Roman military burst into this couple's home one night, destroyed many of their possessions, drove them out onto the street, and ordered them to get out of town. Additionally, it's a good possibility that those marshaled forces also confiscated the couple's legal documents, stripped them of many legal rights, and took away most of their money.

This represented an enormous loss for Aquila and Priscilla financially, mentally, emotionally, and socially. And it was certainly a great loss to them spiritually as well, for they had been forcibly and suddenly severed from their church congregation. It's very likely they didn't have time to tell their families or fellow church members goodbye. In one fell swoop, they had been evicted from their home, isolated from Roman society, and ejected from their home country.

Their Meeting With Paul Was a 'Eureka' Moment

So Aquila and Priscilla began traveling east — not by choice, but rather by force. They probably didn't even know where they were going. Yet, from their home in Rome, Aquila and Priscilla headed for the nearest port, where they boarded a ship that would ultimately take them to Corinth.

When they finally arrived in the city, they must have felt defeated and dejected.

The Bible doesn't tell us whether the couple intended to stay there. Perhaps they had planned to walk to the other side of the city and board another ship to a different Grecian port. But as these two walked the streets of this unfamiliar city, most likely feeling deflated and discouraged, they just "happened" to meet the apostle Paul, who had just arrived in Corinth from Athens. Acts 18:1 and 2 talks about this supernatural meeting:

> **After these things Paul departed from Athens, and came to Corinth; and found a certain Jew named Aquila, born in Pontus, lately come from Italy, with his wife Priscilla; (because that Claudius had commanded all Jews to depart from Rome:) and came unto them.**

Aquila and Priscilla most likely had never even heard of the apostle Paul and, therefore, weren't looking for him. Likewise, Paul wasn't looking for Aquila and Priscilla. But when the paths of these three crossed on the streets of Corinth, it quickly became apparent to them all that it was a divine connection. The Lord had orchestrated the meeting supernaturally, bringing these three people from different parts of the world to converge in the same city, on the same spot, at the same time for the furtherance of His plan and purposes.

The Bible says when Paul arrived in Corinth, he "found" a Jew named Aquila and his wife Priscilla. The word "found" is the Greek word *heurisko*, and it carries an element of *surprise*. It literally means *I found it*, and it is from where we get our word "*eureka.*" When Paul met Aquila and Priscilla in the city of Corinth, it was a *eureka* moment!

In Christ, All Distinctions Disappear

A careful look at Acts 18:2 reveals that the focus was primarily on Aquila. The mention of Priscilla, his wife, is almost an afterthought, which makes sense when we consider the Jewish mindset about women in that day. Many Jewish boys were taught to pray, "I thank God I was not born a woman." Sadly, most Jewish men believed it was better to be born a dog than a woman. But God was in the process of totally changing that mindset.

When God first called Paul, He transplanted him from the church in Jerusalem to the emerging new church in Antioch, which was a melting pot of people from multiple cultures that had been born again into the family of God. Paul — under the inspiration of the Holy Spirit — wrote the most radical, revolutionary statements ever written up until that moment in human history. He said that in the Church...

> ...**There is neither Greek nor Jew, circumcision nor uncircumcision, Barbarian, Scythian, bond nor free: but Christ is all, and in all.**
> — **Colossians 3:11**

> **There is neither Jew nor Greek, there is neither bond nor free, there is neither male nor female: for ye are all one in Christ Jesus.**
> — **Galatians 3:28**

As Paul served as a leader in the church at Antioch, he labored side-by-side with Jews, non-Jews, and Africans. He worked with free men and former slaves, Barbarians and Scythians, men and women. And because all of them were filled and anointed with the Holy Spirit of God, Paul saw firsthand that in Christ, *all distinctions disappear.*

Again, in Paul's day, women had very few rights and were treated very poorly. For example, women were forbidden to shop in the marketplace — only men could shop. If you saw a woman in the marketplace, she was a prostitute. Likewise, most women were not allowed to own property nor could they file for a divorce. To a great degree, women were viewed as property even in the Greek and Roman world.

Therefore, when Paul began to teach that there were no class distinctions in the "new man" created in Christ, it was a radical, revolutionary way of thinking. Skin color, language differences, and gender all evaporated when a person was born of the Spirit into the family of God. That is what Paul was communicating in Colossians 3:11 and Galatians 3:28.

Why Did Paul Say, 'Women Keep Silence in the Churches'?

Now some have thought that the apostle Paul was against women being in ministry based on some of the things he said in his writings. For instance, in First Corinthians 14:34, Paul wrote:

Let your women keep silence in the churches: for it is not permitted unto them to speak; but they are commanded to be under obedience, as also saith the law.

Although on the surface it appears that Paul was saying women shouldn't say anything in church, that was not the case. First, we need to understand the meaning of the word "silence." It is the Greek word *sigao*, and it depicts *a modification of behavior*. In this case, it means *keeping silent* or *keeping control of one's mouth*, as opposed to rambunctiously speaking.

Remember, prior to Paul's teaching, women weren't even allowed in the synagogue. But in Christ, they were welcome to attend church for the first time. Imagine their excitement of being able to attend public meetings with their husbands. At times they were so overwhelmed that they began questioning them about the meaning of what was being said. These conversations the women were trying to carry on with their husbands during the service became quite distracting. To address this issue, Paul told the believers that the women shouldn't keep asking questions during the teaching of the Word. This is made clearer in First Corinthians 14:35, where Paul said:

And if they will learn any thing, let them ask their husbands at home: for it is a shame for women to speak in the church.

Notice the phrase "And if they will learn any thing." In the original Greek, this is the equivalent of saying, *"If, however, they are really longing to seriously learn."* This lets us know that women were excited and coming alive as the Scriptures were being taught. Rather than cause a commotion in the church setting, Paul was merely instructing the women to hold their questions until they returned home. Then they could ask their husbands whatever questions they had.

This brings us to the word "ask" in verse 35. It is a translation of the Greek word *eperotao*, which would better be translated *to interrogate*. It means *to freely ask* and depicts an open conversation. Hence, Paul was saying, "For the women who really want to learn, let them interrogate their husbands at home, not while the Word is being taught. For it is a shame for women to converse and carry on an open conversation during the church service."

What Did Paul Mean by Saying Women Are Not To 'Usurp Authority'?

There is another misunderstood verse regarding women found in First Timothy 2:11. Similarly, it says, "Let the woman learn in silence with all subjection." Again, to understand what Paul was saying here, we have to look at a couple of key words in the original Greek.

For example, the word "learn" in Greek is *manthano*, and it depicts *a learner, a disciple, a follower,* or *an apprentice.* It is from the same root word used to describe the twelve *disciples.* Therefore, when Paul said, "Let the woman learn," he was saying that women can also become *disciples* or *followers* of Jesus. Only they are to become learners in "silence."

Here, the word "silence" does *not* mean speechlessness. It is the Greek word *hesuchia,* and it depicts *a calm behavior — as opposed to an inappropriate or unacceptable behavior.* To this, Paul added, "But I suffer not a woman to teach, nor to usurp authority over the man, but to be in silence" (1 Timothy 2:12). In this verse, the phrase "usurp authority" has often been misinterpreted to mean that women shouldn't preach, but that is not what it means.

In Greek, the word for "usurp authority" is *authenteo,* and it describes *a domineering attitude.* It literally means *to use one's position to take up arms against another, to act as an autocrat.* This word pictures one who, with his own hand, kills others. It carries the idea of using one's position to dominate or to manipulate. In this case, Paul was instructing Timothy not to allow women to have a domineering attitude and take up arms to fight against the "man," which is the Greek word *andros,* meaning *man,* but here, it most likely means *husband.*

The truth is, whether a person is a man or a woman, he or she is not to use their position to dominate or manipulate anyone. A domineering attitude that seeks to take up arms against others is not of God. On the contrary, the Bible says, "Honor Christ by submitting to each other" (Ephesians 5:21 *TLB*). Again, Paul wasn't against women. He was against them usurping authority and trying to dominate their husbands.

Paul's Ministry Team Was Filled With Women

One of the greatest indicators that Paul was a champion of women's rights is the fact that he had many women serving alongside him in ministry.

His closing remarks in his letter to the church at Rome demonstrate this clearly.

In Romans 16:1, he said, "I commend unto you Phebe our sister, which is a servant of the church which is at Cenchrea." The word "servant" here is *diakonon*, which is the Greek term for *a female deacon; a servant with delegated responsibilities that often include public and managerial functions.* Paul said, "...Receive her in the Lord, as becometh saints, and that ye assist her in whatsoever business she hath need of you: for she hath been a succourer of many, and of myself also" (Romans 16:2). Because of Phebe's faithfulness in her responsibilities, Paul instructed the other believers in Rome to stand by and support her in any and all her dealings. He said she was a "succourer" of many, which in Greek means *she was a visible leader, out in front leading others* — she even led Paul at one point.

Paul went on to say, "Greet Priscilla and Aquila my helpers in Christ Jesus" (Romans 16:3). Take note that he mentioned Priscilla *first*, before her husband Aquila. This is actually the way this husband-and-wife team is presented every time they are talked about in Scripture after their introduction in Acts 18. Paul classified them as his "helpers," which is the Greek word *sunergos*, meaning *fellow workers; co-workers; associates;* or *partners.*

Why would Paul call Priscilla and Aquila his "helpers"? He tells us in Romans 16:4 that they "...have for my life laid down their own necks: unto whom not only I give thanks, but also all the churches of the Gentiles."

When we come to Romans 16:7, we see Paul celebrating another husband-and-wife team with whom he was working. He said, "Salute Andronicus and Junia, my kinsmen, and my fellow-prisoners, who are of note among the apostles, who also were in Christ before me." Apparently, these individuals were relatives of Paul who had become Christians before he did, and both — Andronicus and his wife Junia — were apostles. Isn't that significant — a female apostle.

Paul then added, "Salute Tryphena and Tryphosa, who labour in the Lord..." (Romans 16:12). These two were twin sisters who worked in ministry with Paul. Furthermore, he urged the Roman believers to "Salute Philologus, and Julia, Nereus, and his sister, and Olympas, and all the saints which are with them" (Romans 16:15). Here again, we see two more women — Julia and Olympas — serving in ministry side by side with Paul.

All these verses in Romans 16 confirm that the apostle Paul was *for* women, not against them. There is no way he would have worked with so many of them in ministry and then included them in his writings had he not believed that they are truly equal with men and a play a vital role in advancing God's kingdom.

Priscilla was one of these powerful women with whom Paul was privileged to work. The Bible says that once he connected with her and her husband, Aquila, "…He abode with them, and wrought…" (Acts 18:3). The word "wrought" is taken from the Greek word *poieo*, and it denotes *creativity*. Therefore, when these three met, they immediately swung into action, *creatively* and energetically working together with all their hearts to preach the Gospel and equip new believers in their faith.

Even though Priscilla and Aquila's expulsion from Rome was heartbreaking and it appeared that all was lost, God's promise in Romans 8:28 came true: "And we know that all things work together for good to them that love God, to them who are the called according to his purpose." That is what God did in the lives of Priscilla, Aquila, and Paul, and it is what you can trust Him to do in your life too!

STUDY QUESTIONS

> Study to shew thyself approved unto God, a workman that needeth
> not to be ashamed, rightly dividing the word of truth.
> — 2 Timothy 2:15

1. What interesting new details did you discover about Priscilla and Aquila? What is most fascinating to you about this husband-and-wife ministry team? Why?

2. In your own words, explain what Paul meant and why he said:
    - "…Women keep silence in the churches: for it is not permitted unto them to speak…" (1 Corinthians 14:34).
    - "Let the woman learn in silence… I suffer not a woman to teach, nor to usurp authority over the man, but to be in silence" (1 Timothy 2:11,12).

3. Under the inspiration and direction of the Holy Spirit, the apostle Paul declared that in Christ, all distinctions disappear (*see* Colossians 3:11; Galatians 3:28). Skin color, language differences, and gender all

evaporate in God's family. Be honest: Do you agree with this truth, or does it challenge your perspective?

PRACTICAL APPLICATION

But be ye doers of the word, and not hearers only,
deceiving your own selves.
—James 1:22

1. Aquila and Priscilla — and many other Jewish believers living in Rome during the reign of Claudius — suffered religious persecution in that they were forcefully ejected from their homes because of their belief in Christ. Have you suffered religious persecution on your job, in school, or in your community? If so, briefly share what took place.

2. How is God taking your discouraging ordeal and working it together for your good? What positive outcomes are being produced as a result?

3. Prior to this lesson, what was your view of women being actively involved in ministry? What have you learned in this lesson that has helped expand your understanding and bring greater clarity on the subject?

4. The fact that Paul and Aquila and Priscilla met in the city of Corinth was not an accident. It was an amazing "eureka" moment for all three. With whom has God divinely connected you to do life — and possibly ministry? What were the supernatural circumstances that God orchestrated to bring you together? If you have never experienced a divine connection of this nature, pray and ask the Lord to connect you with the right person (or people) at the right time that will help you fulfill God's call on your life.

Notes

Notes